KETO AIR FRYER COOKBOOK FOR BEGINNERS

Simple & Delicious Ketogenic

Air Fryer Recipes for Healthy Living

MARY NELSON

Copyright © 2019 by Mary Nelson

All rights reserved. No part of this publication may be reproduced, distributed or transmitted in any form or by any means, including photocopying, recording, or other electronic or mechanical methods, without the prior written permission of the publisher, except in the case of brief quotations embodied in critical reviews and certain other noncommercial uses permitted by copyright law.

Limit of liability/Disclaimer of Warranty: The publisher and the author make no representation or warranties with respect to the accuracy or completeness of the contents of this work and specifically disclaim all warranties, including without limitation warranties of fitness for a particular purpose. NO warranty may be created or extended by sales or promotional materials. The advice and strategies contained herein may not be suitable for every situation. This work is sold with the understanding that the author is not engaged in rendering medical, legal or other professional advice or services. If professional assistance is required, the services of a competent professional person should be sought. Neither the publisher nor the author shall be liable for damages arising herefrom. The fact that an individual, organization, or website is referred to in this work as a citation and/or potential source of further information does not mean that the author or the publisher endorses the information the individual, organization or website may provide or recommendations they/it may make.

.ISBN-13: 978- 1691187553

DEDICATION

To all who desire to live life to the fullest!

TABLE OF CONTENT

INTRODUCTION 1

THE KETO DIET 3

Benefits of a Keto Diet 3

THE AIR FRYER 5

Benefits of an Air Fryer 5

Components of the Air Fryer 6

How to handle the Air Fryer 7

BREAKFAST RECIPES 9

Air Fried Keto Paleo Baked Chicken 9

Coffee & Spice Ribeye with Air Fryer 11

Cheese mix with Creamy Almond 13

Air Fryer Carne Asada 14

Breakfast Bacon 16

Delicious Turkey Buke 17

Air Fried Pork Chops 18

Hard Boiled Eggs 19

Bacon Eggs cups 20

Spinach Pie 21

Egg mix with Tomatoes 22

Delicious Cinnamon Toast 23

Beef Kabobs 24

Eggplant with chives 25

Cloud Eggs 26

Bell Peppers and Eggs 27

Chinese-style Spareribs 28

Breakfast Beans Oatmeal.. 29

Delicious Strawberry Oatmeal.. 30

Breakfast Carrot Oatmeal 31

Delicious Apple Oatmeal 32

Breakfast Pumpkin Oatmeal 33

Roasted Asian broccoli 34

Roast Beef 36

Egg Muffins 37

Biscuits Casserole 38

Chicken Tenders 39

Air Fried Parsnip Hash Browns 40

Buffalo Wings 42

Breakfast Sandwich 43

Spicy Bacon 44

Fried Parmesan Zucchini 45

Herbed Tomatoes... 46

Spicy Bacon Bites.. 47

Mac and Cheese 48

Radish Hash Browns with Air Fryer 49

Pan de Yuca (Colombian) 50

Tomato and Eggs 51

LUNCH RECIPES.. 53

Chicken Jalfrezi 53

Cilantro Pesto Chicken Legs... 55

Mascarpone Mushroom Pasta 56

Korean Chicken Wings...57

Spicy Pepper Scotch Eggs 59

Fried Cheesecake Bites 60

Steak Nuggets with a white barbecue sauce 61

Vietnamese Grilled Pork Thit Nuong 63

Spicy Jicama Fries..64

Garlic Butter Naan Bread 65

Buffalo Cauliflower..67

Brazilian Chicken 68

Tomato Basil Scallops...69

Cauliflower Rice..70

Honey roasted carrots 71

Chicken Parmesan 72

Indian Kheema Meatloaf..74

Indian Spicy Fennel Chicken 75

Salmon Bok Choy...77

Fried Pickles...79

Cornish hen..80

Hot Dogs...81

Southern Fried Catfish...82

Tijuana Street Taco 83

Chicken Without Gluten 85

Steak Bites..86

DINNER RECIPES 89

Blue Cheese Ribeye Steak...89

Buffalo Chicken Legs 90

Zesty Ranch Air Fryer Fish Fillets 91

Crispy Pork Belly 92

Turkey Breast Tenderloin 93

Smoked BBQ Ribs 94

Brussels Sprouts 95

Garlic Parmesan Breaded Fried Chicken Wings 96

Fried Chicken 97

Crispy Veggie Fries 99

Monkey Bread 100

Mozzarella Cheese Sticks 101

Chanukkah Latkes 102

Eggplant Parmesan 103

Chicken Wings (Plain) 105

Chicken Wings (Parmesan) 106

French Fries 107

Popcorn Chicken 108

Orange Turkey Burgers 109

Persian Kabab Koobideh 111

Garlic Ranch Wings 113

SIDE DISH RECIPES 115

Cauliflower Rice 115

Herbed Brussels Sprouts 116

Scotch Eggs with Spicy Pepper Sauce 117

Buffalo Chicken Bites 119

Chicken Coconut Meatballs 120

Avocado fries *121*

Buffalo Cauliflower Bites *122*

Parmesan Meatballs *123*

Baked Potato - Baked Garlic Parsley Potatoes *124*

Zero Oil Crispy Roasted Broccoli *125*

Corn on the Cob *126*

Breaded Mushrooms *127*

Shrimp Toast (Chinese) *128*

Salmon Croquettes (Jewish style) *130*

Passover Matzo Taco Chips *131*

Garlic Bread Buns *132*

Sweet Potato Fries *133*

Peanut Butter Banana Dessert Bites *134*

INTRODUCTION

If you have an Air Fryer, you already know it is a very important kitchen appliance that saves you a lot of time cooking. If you have not gotten an Air Fryer, it will intrigue you to know that the Air Fryer replaces deep frying. It cooks food by circulating hot air around it thereby requiring just a few drops of oil, cutting down fats and amazingly the Air Fryer offers various cooking options, making it possible to cook your favorite meals with it.

The Keto diet is a low carb diet that makes you burn lot of fats and also prevents some illness, just imagine eating healthy meals that makes you the Air Fryer.

This book introduces you to the Keto Diet and a comprehensive list of easy-to-make recipes making you have something delicious to cook at every time with a variety in taste, keeping you fit and healthy at the same time. Also, you will learn everything you need to know about how and why to use the Air Fryer. Let's get started!

THE KETO DIET

The Keto diet is a low carb diet high on fat and moderate in protein which makes the body switch from using fat to using Carbohydrates and in turn makes the body burn fats effortlessly. Ketogenic meals are delicious and rich because there are a lot of ingredients you are allowed to use.

Scientists have noted that fat is responsible for weight gain which is associated with illness like diabetes, obesity and epilepsy in children. The Keto diet is all you need to live that healthy life without sacrificing on taste.

Benefits of a Keto Diet

The Keto diet is no ordinary Diet, listed are some of the benefits attached to the keto Diet

- Weight Loss
- Reduce risk of Cancer
- Improves Heart Health
- Reduce Blood Sugar
- Antiaging
- Lower Blood Pressure

- Improves Brain function
- Clearer Skin

THE AIR FRYER

Not only are the ingredients important, but so too is the method in which you use to prepare your meals. The Air Fryer has proven to be a must have kitchen appliance for every home as With the Air Fryer, you can make all your favorite dishes in an absolutely healthy way. It replaces and is healthier than deep frying as it cuts down fats, instead of using gallons of oil, the Air Fryer needs only a few drops.

The Air Fryer ensures food is cooked through the circulation of hot air in the chamber. There is a mechanical fan present in the Air Fryer that circulates this hot air at high speed around the food. Also, with the Air Fryer, you can cook, fry, roast, grill and sauté.

Benefits of an Air Fryer

Here are some of the benefits of the Air Fryer:

- Easy to clean
- Healthy
- Saves time
- Easy to use
- Saves space

- Multi-cooking options

Components of the Air Fryer

Are you new to using the Air Fryer? You need to understand these components to use it properly.

Air Fryer Basket: This is also known as the cooking chamber. It usually has coated metal sides and a mesh bottom. it is where the cooking takes place and its look varies on brand. Some brand has racks. Regardless of the brand of Air Fryer you have, these recipes are compatible with them

Coil: This is also known as the heating element because it produces the heat using the electricity passing through it. The air is pushed through the coil once it reaches the temperature you want.

Fan: The fan is responsible for the circulation of air and keeping it super-heated to get your food crispy. This is the component that cooks your food.

Exhaust System: The exhaust system gets rid of harmful build-up of excess pressure, unpleasant odour and dirt so that they don't affect your food

How to handle the Air Fryer

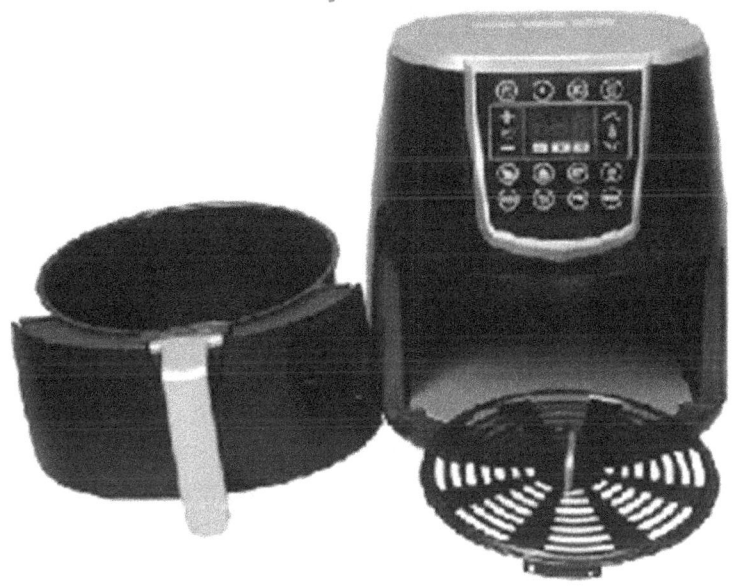

If you are new to the Air Fryer, it is very important you handle the Air Fryer rightly making it easier for you to cook the recipes. These tips are extremely useful

Use Oils:

Remember that you are on the Keto diet, so the oil you use should be keto friendly. Olive oil, Coconut oil or non-sticky oil depending on the recipe. Vegetable oil should be avoided.

Preheat Air Fryer

Using the Air Fryer requires you preheating the Air Fryer most of the time. Make sure you check and follow the Recipes Procedures. The benefit of preheating the Air Fryer is to ensure you don't cook your food before its hot enough to really crisp it.

Grease the Basket

Greasing the Basket is very important if you don't want the food to slip, even if you are coating the food in oil, the basket still needs to be greased to ensure the "breading" stays in place. Always follow the procedures with each recipe.

Wait before cleaning

Before you clean the Air Fryer, wait for it to completely cool after you turn it off. The Air Fryer does not cool down too easily, you have to give it adequate cooling time. An average of 30 minutes is required before cleaning.

Pay attention to Cook Time and Temperature

Follow the Procedures is each recipe squarely. Each recipe vary in cooking time and cook temperature and it should be appropriately observed as it provides the food with the required doneness. For crispness, it might be required you cook for additional cooking time as stated in the recipe

BREAKFAST RECIPES

Air Fried Keto Paleo Baked Chicken

Preparation Time: 10 minutes

Cook Time: 15 minutes

Serving: 4

Ingredients

- 4 Egg whites
- 1 Pound of boneless, skinless chicken breast
- 6 Tablespoon of Toasted sesame seeds
- 1/4 Cup of Coconut flour
- 1 Teaspoon of Sesame oil
- Pinch sea salt
- 1/2 Teaspoon of Ground Ginger
- Nonstick cooking spray

For the dip:

- 1 Tablespoon Water

- 2 Tablespoon of Natural creamy almond butter
- 2 Teaspoon of Rice vinegar
- 4 Teaspoon of Coconut aminos
- 1/2 Teaspoon of Ground ginger
- Sriracha to taste

Procedures

1. Heat the Air Fryer for 10 minutes (400 degrees)

2. Chop the Chicken to Nuggets

Note: About 1-inch pieces

3. Dry the Chicken Nuggets and place them in a bowl.

4. Toss with the sesame oil and salt until coated

5. Put the Ground Ginger and Coconut flour in a zipped bag then shake.

6. Add the Chicken also and shake until coated

7. Place the eggs in a large bowl and add the chicken nuggets.

8. Mix until they are well coated in the egg.

9. Put the Sesame seeds in a zip bag.

10. Shake off any excess egg from the chicken and put the chicken nuggets into the same bag as the sesame seed.

11. Shake until well coated

12. Spray the Air Fryer Basket with cooking spray and put the nuggets into the basket. Spray little cooking spray.

13. Cook for 6 minutes. Flip the nuggets and spray for cooking spray.

14. Cook for another 5 minutes until it is no longer pink inside, with a crispy outside.

15. Mix all the sauce ingredients together in a medium bowl until smooth.

16. Serve the Nuggets with the dip and Devour.

Nutritional Information: 346kcal | Fat: 19g | Carbs: 6g | Protein: 36g

Coffee & Spice Ribeye with Air Fryer

Preparation Time: 25 minutes

Cook Time: 9 minutes

Servings: 2

Ingredients

- 1 lb. Ribeye steak
- 1/4 Teaspoon of Powdered Onion
- 1/2 Teaspoon of Ground Coffee
- 1 1/2 Teaspoon Coarse Sea Salt
- 1/4 Teaspoon of Chili Powder
- 1/4 Teaspoon of Powdered Chipotle
- 1/2 Teaspoon of Black Pepper
- 1/4 Teaspoon of Powdered Garlic
- 1/4 Teaspoon of Paprika
- 1/8 Teaspoon of Coriander
- 1/8 Teaspoon of Cocoa Powder
- 1 Teaspoon of Brown Sugar

Procedures

1. Whisk all spices in a bowl.

Note: Make sure to break up the pesky brown sugar

2. Sprinkle a reasonable amount of the spice mix onto a plate and lay one steak on top of spices.

3. Season the steak with spice mix and evenly rub into meat.

Note: Flip to make sure the other side is seasoned properly.

4. Take Steak and press all sides into the remaining spice mix on the plate in order to avoid the spices wasting.

5. Allow steak to come to room temperature by letting it sit for at least 20 minutes.

6. Coat Air Fryer basket with oil and heat to 390 degrees for at least 3 minutes.

7. Cook the steak for 9 minutes.

Note: Do not flip or open!!

8. Once cook time is finished, remove and let it rest for at least 5 minutes before slicing.

9. Serve

Nutritional Information: 495kcal | Fat: 32g | Carbohydrate: 5g | Protein: 46g

Cheese mix with Creamy Almond

Preparation Time: 10 minutes

Cook Time: 20 minutes

Servings: 6

Ingredients

- 6 Eggs, whisked
- 9 Oz soft cream cheese
- 1 Cup almond milk
- 6 Spring onions, chopped
- 1 Cup cheddar cheese, shredded
- Salt and black pepper to taste
- Cooking spray

Procedures

1. Preheat the Air Fryer with the oil at 350F and grease with the cooking spray

2. Mix the Eggs with the remaining ingredients in a bowl. Whisk thoroughly!

3. Pour the mixture into the Air Fryer and cook for 20 minutes.

Divide and Serve!

Nutritional Information: 231kcal | Fat: 11g | Carbs: 5g | Protein: 8g

Air Fryer Carne Asada

Preparation Time: 10 mins

Cook Time: 8 mins

Servings: 4

Ingredients

- 2 Medium limes juiced
- 1 Teaspoon of coriander seeds
- 1 Cup of cilantro
- 1.5 Pounds skirt steak
- 1 Medium orange peeled and seeded
- 1 Teaspoon of cumin seeds
- 2 Teaspoons of sugar
- 1 Diced jalapeno
- 2 Tablespoons of vinegar
- 2 Teaspoons of powder
- 2 Tablespoons of vegetable oil
- 1 Teaspoon of salt

Procedures

1.Put all ingredients except the skirt steak in a blender and blend to a smooth sauce

2. Cut the Steak into four pieces and put into a zip-top plastic bag.

3. Pour the marinade on the steak and allow meat to marinate for 30 minutes or for 24 hours in the Fridge

4. Set Air Fryer to 400F and put steak in the basket.

5. Cook for 8 minutes.

Note: Do not Overcook!

6. Let Steak simmer for 10 minutes.

7. Slice the steak against the grain

Serve!

Nutritional Information: 330kcal | Fat: 19g | Carbs: 1g | Protein: 37g

Breakfast Bacon

Preparation Time: 3 minutes

Cook Time: 11 minutes

Servings: 11 slices

Ingredients

- 11 Slices of bacon

Procedures

1. Divide Bacon into halves and place the first half in the Air Fryer

2. Set Air Fryer to 400F and cook for 10 minutes [Lesser time for thinner bacon]

3. Check after 5 minutes with a tong to confirm if anything needs to be rearranged

4. Cook to desired doneness. [Extra 2 minutes for extra crispy]

Serve

Nutritional Information: 91kcal | Fat: 8g | Carbs: 0g | Protein: 2g

Delicious Turkey Bake

Preparation Time: 5 minutes

Cook Time: 25 minutes

Servings: 4

Ingredients

- 2 Eggs, whisked
- 1 Turkey breast, skinless and boneless, cut into strips and browned
- 2 Cups cheddar cheese, shredded
- 1 Tablespoon chopped chives
- 2 Cups Almond milk
- 2 Teaspoon Olive oil
- Salt and Pepper to taste

Procedures

1. Mix the eggs with milk, cheese, salt, pepper and the chives in a bowl, whisk well

2. Preheat Air Fryer at 330F

3. Add The oil, heat it up.

4. Add the Turkey pieces, spread well.

5. Add the eggs mixture, toss a bit and cook for 25 minutes.

Serve!!

Nutritional Information: 224kcal | Fat: 11g | Carbs: 5g | Protein: 7g

Air Fried Pork Chops

Preparation Time: 5 minutes

Cook Time: 16 minutes

Servings: 4

Ingredients

- 4 Boneless pork chops
- 1/2 Teaspoon of parsley4
- 1/2 Teaspoon of celery seed
- 1/4 Teaspoon of sugar
- 2 Teaspoons of oil
- 1/2 Teaspoon garlic, granulated
- 1/2 Teaspoon of salt
- 1/2 Teaspoon onion, granulated

Procedures

1. Mix the seasonings together and sprinkle them on all sides of the pork chops

2. Rub the oil in on the pork chops, use of spray oil recommended

3. Cook at 350F for 10 minutes (for thin) and 16 minutes (for thick)

NOTE: Flip to other side midway through the cooking time

4. Pork Chops are done once it reaches 145F measured in the center. For well-done Pork chops, go to 156F.

Serve

Hard Boiled Eggs

Preparation Time: 2 minutes

Cook Time: 15 minutes

Servings: 6

Ingredients

- 6 Eggs

Procedures

1. Place the eggs in the Air Fryer Basket and at 260F for 15 minutes

2. Once time is expired, remove eggs and put in an ice water bath for 10 minutes

Serve as desired

Nutritional Information: 78kcal | Fat: 5g | Carbs: 0.5g | Protein: 6g

Bacon Eggs cups

Preparation Time: 10 minutes

Cooking Time: 15 minutes

Servings: 4

Ingredients

- 4 Eggs
- 1/2 Teaspoon dried dill
- 6 Oz Bacon
- 1 Tablespoon butter
- 1/4 Teaspoon salt
- 1/2 Teaspoon Paprika

Procedures

1. Crack the egg in a bowl and mix with salt, paprika and dried dill, preferably with a hand mixer

2. Grease 4 ramekins with butter.

3. Slice the Bacons and put it in the prepared ramekins in the shape of cups then pour the egg mixture in the middle of each bacon cup.

4. Set the Air Fryer to 360F and put the ramekins in it then cook for 15 minutes.

5. Remove and serve!

Nutritional Information: 319kcal | Fat: 25.1g | Carbs: 1.2g | Protein: 21.4g

Spinach Pie

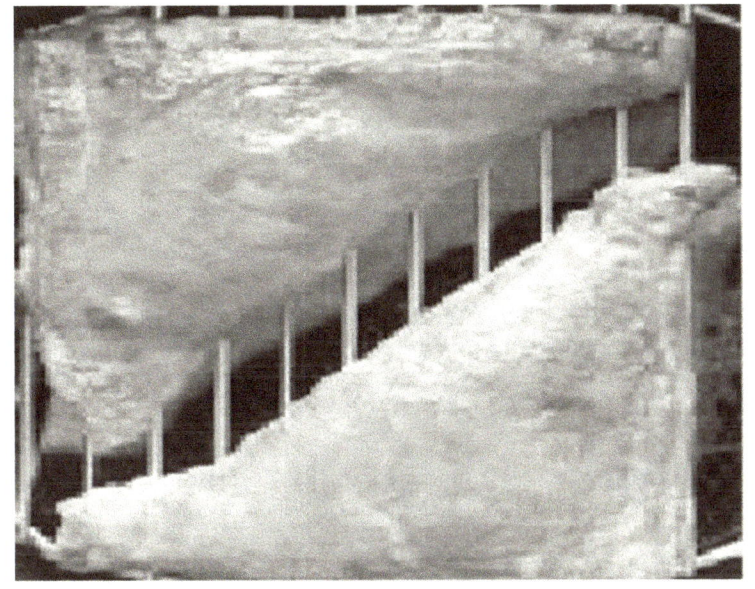

Preparation Time: 15 minutes

Cooking Time: 19 minutes

Servings: 4

Ingredients

- 7 Oz torn Spinach
- 2 whisked Eggs
- 7 Oz white flour
- 3 Oz crumbled mozzarella cheese
- 2 Tablespoons milk
- 2 Tablespoons Olive oil
- 1 red onion, chopped
- Salt and black pepper to taste

Procedures

1. Mix flour with 1 tablespoon of olive oil, milk, eggs, salt and pepper in a food processor. Pulse, then transfer to a bowl.

2. Knead the mixture a bit then cover and keep in the fridge for 10 minutes.

3. Heat up a Pan using the remaining oil over medium heat and then add all the remaining ingredients.

4. Stir and cook for 4 minutes.

5. Divide the dough into 4 pieces, roll each piece and place in the bottom of a ramekin.

6. Divide the Spinach mixture evenly between the ramekins then place in the air fryer and cook for 15 minutes at 360F

Serve!!

Nutritional Information: 200kcal | Fat: 12g | Carbs: 13g | Protein: 5g

Egg mix with Tomatoes

Preparation Time: 5 minutes

Cook Time: 25 minutes

Servings: 4

Ingredients

- 6 Eggs, whisked
- 30 Oz canned tomatoes, chopped
- 2 Tablespoons chives, chopped
- 2 Tablespoons olive oil
- 1/2 Pound cheddar, shredded
- Salt and black pepper to taste

Procedures

1. Add the oil and preheat the Air Fryer at 350F

2. Add the tomatoes, eggs, salt and pepper and whisk.

3. Add the cheese on top and sprinkle the chives on top.

4. Cook for 25 minutes

Divide and Serve

Nutritional Information: 221kcal | Fat: 8g | Carbs: 4g | Protein: 8g

Delicious Cinnamon Toast

Preparation Time: 15 minutes

Cook Time: 5 minutes

Servings: 6

Ingredients

- 12 Slices of bread
- 1 and 1/2 tablespoon cinnamon
- 1 Stick butter
- 1 and 1/2 tablespoon Vanilla extract
- 1/2 Cup sugar
- Pepper to taste

Procedures

1. Mix butter, sugar, pepper and vanilla extract in a microwave proof bowl.

2. Warm the mixture and stir for 30 seconds until everything melts then pour the mixture over the bread slices.

3. Put the Bread slices in the Air Fryer basket and cook at 400F for 5 minutes.

4. Serve with Fresh banana and berry sauce.

Nutritional Information: 281kcal | Fat: 5g | Carbs: 18g | Protein: 3g

Beef Kabobs

Preparation Time: 30 minutes

Cook Time: 10 minutes

Servings: 3

Ingredients

- 1 Bell peppers
- 1 lb beef chuck ribs cut in 1-inch pieces
- 1/3 Cup of low-fat sour cream
- 2 Tablespoon of soy sauce
- 8 (6) Inch skewers
- 1/2 Onion

Procedures

1. Mix the sour cream with the soy sauce in a medium bowl and place the beef chunks inside and marinate for a minimum of 30 minutes (Preferably overnight)

2. Cut the bell pepper and onion into 1-inch pieces.

3. Soak the skewers in water for about 10 minutes

4. Thread the beef, onions and bell peppers onto skewers.

5. Add some freshly ground black pepper and cook at 400F for 10 minutes. Turn after the first 5 minutes

Nutritional Information: 250kcal | Fat: 15g | Carbs: 4g | Protein: 23g

Eggplant with chives

Preparation Time: 5 minutes

Cook Time: 20 minutes

Servings: 4

Ingredients

- 2 Tablespoons chives, chopped
- 3 Eggplants
- 2 Teaspoon paprika(sweet)
- 2 Tablespoon Olive oil
- Salt and black pepper to taste

Procedures

1. Cook the Eggplants in the Air Fryer for 20 minutes at 380F

2. Peel the Eggplant, blend in a blender with the remaining ingredients. Pulse well.

Divide and Serve

Nutritional Information: 190kcal | Fat: 7g | Carbs: 5g | Protein: 3g

Cloud Eggs

Preparation Time: 8 minutes

Cook Time: 4 minutes

Servings: 2

Ingredients

- 2 eggs
- 1 Teaspoon butter

Procedures

1. Separate the egg whites and egg yolks into separate bowls.

2. Whisk the egg whites with a hand mixer until you get strong white peaks.

3. Grease the Air Fryer basket with butter and preheat to 300F.

4. Make medium clouds from the egg white peaks in the Air Fryer basket and place the basket in the Air Fryer.

5. Cook cloud eggs for 2 minutes.

6. Remove the basket and place the egg yolks in the center of every egg cloud, return back inside the air fryer

7. Cook for 2 minutes.

8. Remove and serve!

Bell Peppers and Eggs

Preparation Time: 5 minutes

Cook Time: 20 minutes

Servings: 4

Ingredients

- 4 Eggs, whisked
- 1 Red bell pepper (cut into strips)
- 1 Green bell pepper (cut into strips)
- 1 Orange bell pepper (cut into strips)
- 2 Tablespoons shredded mozzarella
- Salt and pepper to taste
- Cooking Spray of choice

Procedures

1. Mix the Eggs and all the bell peppers, with salt and pepper in a bowl and toss.

2. Preheat Air Fryer at 350F.

3. Grease the Air Fryer basket with cooking spray and pour in the egg mixture, spread then sprinkle the mozzarella on top.

4. Cook for 20 minutes.'

Divide and serve!!

Nutritional Information: 229kcal | Fat: 13g | Carbs: 4g | Protein: 7g

Chinese-style Spareribs

Preparation Time: 40 minutes

Cook Time: 10 minutes

Servings: 4

Ingredients

- 1 Tablespoon of fermented black bean paste
- 1 Tablespoon of sesame oil
- 1 Tablespoon of honey
- 1.5 Pounds of spareribs cut into small pieces
- 1 Teaspoon of garlic, minced
- 1 Tablespoon of dark soy sauce
- 1 Teaspoon ginger, minced
- 1 Tablespoon of wine

Procedures

1. Stir together all Marinade ingredients in a large bowl

2. Add the spare ribs to the mixture and mix. (Allow it to marinade for at least 30 minutes or up to 20 hours)

3. Once you are ready to cook the ribs, remove the ribs from the marinade and cook in the Air Fryer at 375F for 8 minutes

Ensure the ribs have internal temperature of 165F before Serving

Nutritional Information: 386kcal | Fat: 31g | Carbs: 4g | Protein: 18g

Breakfast Beans Oatmeal

Preparation Time: 5 minutes

Cook Time: 15 minutes

Servings: 2

Ingredients

- 2 Tablespoons canned kidney beans, drained
- 1 Cup steel cut Oats
- 4 Tablespoons heavy cream
- 2 red bell papers, chopped
- 1/4 Teaspoon cumin, ground
- Salt and Pepper to taste

Procedures

1. Preheat Air Fryer to 360F

2. Add all ingredients, toss and cover.

3. Cook for 15 minutes.

4. Divide into bowls and serve

Nutritional Information: 203kcal | Fat: 4g | Carbs: 12g | Protein: 4g

Delicious Strawberry Oatmeal

Preparation Time: 5 minutes

Cook Time: 10 minutes

Servings: 4

Ingredients

- 1 Cup steel cut Oats
- 1 Cup Strawberries, chopped
- 1 Cup almond milk
- 1/2 Teaspoon vanilla extract
- 2 Tablespoon Sugar
- Cooking spray

Procedures

1. Spray Air Fryer with cooking spray.

2. Add all ingredients, toss and cover.

3. Cook for 10 minutes at 365F.

4. Divide into bowls and serve

Nutritional Information: 172kcal | Fat: 6g | Carbs: 11g | Protein: 5g

Breakfast Carrot Oatmeal

Preparation Time: 5 minutes

Cook Time: 15 minutes

Servings: 4

Ingredients

- 1/2 Cup steel cut Oats
- 1 Cup Carrots, shredded
- 2 Cups milk of choice
- 1 Teaspoon Cardamom, ground
- 2 Tablespoon Sugar
- Cooking spray

Procedures

1. Spray Air Fryer with cooking spray.

2. Add all ingredients, toss and cover.

3. Cook for 15 minutes at 365F.

4. Divide into bowls and serve

Nutritional Information: 172kcal | Fat: 7g | Carbs: 14g | Protein: 5g

Delicious Apple Oatmeal

Preparation Time: 5 minutes

Cook Time: 15 minutes

Servings: 6

Ingredients

- 1 and 1/4 Cups steel cut oats
- 2 Apples, cored, peeled and chopped
- 1/4 Teaspoon allspice, ground
- 2 Teaspoon Sugar
- 3 Cups Almond milk
- 1/4 Teaspoon cardamom, ground
- 1/2 Cinnamon powder
- 2 Teaspoon Vanilla extract
- 1/4 teaspoon nutmeg, ground
- 1/4 teaspoon ginger powder
- Cooking spray

Procedures

1. Spray Air Fryer with cooking spray.

2. Add all the ingredients and stir.

3. cover and cook for 15 minutes at 15 minutes

4. Divide into bowls and serve

Nutritional Information: 212kcal | Fat: 5g | Carbs: 14g | Protein: 5g

Breakfast Pumpkin Oatmeal

Preparation Time: 5 minutes

Cook Time: 20 minutes

Servings: 4

Ingredients

- 1 Teaspoon Pumpkin pie spice
- 1/2 Cup steel cut Oats
- 1/2 Cup Pumpkin puree
- 1 and 1/2 Cups milk
- 3 Tablespoon Sugar

Procedures

1. Mix all ingredients in the Air fryer. Stir and cook for 20 minutes at 360F

2. Divide into bowls and serve

Nutritional Information: 141kcal | Fat: 4g | Carbs: 8g | Protein: 5g

Roasted Asian broccoli

Preparation Time: 10 minutes

Cook Time: 20 minutes

Servings: 4

Ingredients

- 1 Lb Broccoli, Cut into florets
- 2 Tablespoon Reduced sodium soy sauce
- 1/3 Cup of Roasted salted peanuts
- 2 Teaspoons of Sriracha
- 1 Tablespoon of minced Garlic
- Salt as desired
- 1 1/2 Tablespoon of Peanut oil
- 1 Teaspoon of Rice vinegar
- 2 Teaspoon Honey
- Fresh lime juice (optional)

Procedures

1. Mix the Peanut oil, Broccoli and garlic in a large bowl

2. Season the mixture with salt and ensure the oil covers the broccoli florets. you can use hands to give a quick rub for each of the broccoli florets

3. Place Broccoli into the Air fryer basket and spread in as single of a layer.

Note: Leave a bit of space between the florets

4. Cook at a temperature of 400 degrees for 20 minutes until crispy and golden brown. Stir after the first 10 minutes.

5. Mix together the soy sauce, rice vinegar and the honey in a small bowl

6. Put the mixture in a microwave for 15 seconds till the honey is properly melted

7. Add the soy sauce mixture and to the cooked broccoli in a bowl.

8. Toss to coat and season with very little salt to taste.

9. Stir the peanuts in the mixture

10. If desired, Squeeze lime on top

Serve!!!!

Roast Beef

Preparation Time: 5 minutes

Cook Time: 45 minutes

Servings: 4

Ingredients

- 1 Tablespoon of olive oil
- 2 lb. Beef roast
- 1 Teaspoon of rosemary
- 1 Teaspoon of salt

Procedures

1. Preheat the Air Fryer to 360F

2. Mix all the ingredients on a plate except the beef

3. Place the beef on the plate of the mixture and turn until the mixture coats the outside

4. Place in Air Fryer and cook for 45 minutes

5. Once done, remove from Air Fryer and cover with kitchen foil then allow to simmer for ten minutes before serving

Cut against the grain

Nutritional Information: 293kcal | Fat: 19g | Protein: 29g

Egg Muffins

Preparation Time: 10 minutes

Cook Time: 15 minutes

Servings: 4

Ingredients

- 1 Egg
- 2 Oz grated Parmesan
- 3 Tablespoon milk
- 1 Tablespoon of baking powder
- Splash of Worcestershire sauce
- Oz of white flour
- 2 Tablespoon of Olive Oil

Procedures

1. Mix the Eggs with flour, baking powder, oil, milk, parmesan and Worcestershire in a bowl. Whisk well and divide into 4 silicon muffin cups.

2. Arrange the cups in the Air Fryer basket, cook for 15 minutes at 392F.

Serve!!

Nutritional Information: 251kcal | Fat: 6g | Carbs: 9g | Protein: 3g

Biscuits Casserole

Preparation Time: 10 minutes

Cook Time: 15 minutes

Servings: 8

Ingredients

- 12 Oz biscuits, quartered
- 2 and 1/2 Cups milk
- 1/2 Pound Sausage, chopped
- 3 Tablespoons flour
- Cooking spray of choice
- Salt and black pepper to taste

Procedures

1. Grease Air Fryer with spray and preheat at 350F.

2. Add the biscuits on the bottom and mix with the sausage.

3. Add the flour, milk, salt and pepper, toss a bit and cook for 15 minutes.

4. Divide and serve!

Nutritional Information: 321kcal | Fat: 4g | Carbs: 12g | Protein: 5g

Chicken Tenders

Preparation Time: 8 minutes

Cook Time: 10 minutes

Servings: 2

Ingredients

- 1-1/2 lbs. Chicken tenders
- 1 Teaspoon of fine sea salt
- 1/2 Teaspoon of ground black pepper
- 2 Tablespoon of ground flax seed
- 1/2 Teaspoon of powdered garlic
- 1/2 Teaspoon of powdered onion
- 2 Eggs
- 1 Teaspoon of Italian seasoning
- 1 Teaspoon of paprika
- 1 Cup fine of almond flour
- Avocado oil spray

Procedures

1. Heat the Air Fryer to 400F

2. Whisk the eggs in a bowl

3. Mix the almond flour, flaxseed and all the seasonings till they are properly mixed

4. Dip the sliced chicken into the egg mixture and dredge it inside the first mixture of the flour.

Repeat the process till all the chickens are coated.

5. Grease the Air Fryer basket with the avocado spray

6. Place the chickens in the basket with plenty of space between them.

7. Lightly rub the chicken with avocado spray

8. Fry for 10 minutes, flip halfway through

Repeat the process with the remaining chicken till they are coated

Serve

Nutritional Information: *299*kcal | Fat: 19g | Carbs: 7g | Protein: 25g

Air Fried Parsnip Hash Browns

Preparation Time: 20 minutes

Cook Time: 15 minutes

Servings: 2

Ingredients

- 3 Eggs, beaten
- 1 Large parsnip, grated
- 1 Cup flour
- 1/2 Teaspoon garlic powder
- 1/4 Teaspoon nutmeg
- 1 Tablespoon Olive Oil
- Salt and pepper to taste

Procedures

1. Heat the Olive oil in the Air Fryer at 390F

2. Combine the remaining ingredients and season with salt and pepper.

3. Form patties out of the mixture and arrange in the Air Fryer.

4. Cook for 15 minutes.

Nutritional Information: 507kcal | Fat: 14.8g | Carbs: 74.2g | Protein: 18.3g

Buffalo Wings

Preparation time: 5 minutes

Cook time: 20 minutes

Servings: 2

Ingredients

- 1/4 Cup of your favorite Keto Hot Sauce
- 1 lb. Chicken wings/drumettes
- Nonstick oil spray
- 1 Tablespoon of grass-fed butter

Procedures

1. Preheat Air Fryer to 400F.

2. In a small saucepan over medium heat, melt the butter and add in the hot sauce then whisk until fully combined.

3. Turn the heat down to low and keep the sauce warm

4. Add the Chicken wings to the Air Fryer and spray lightly with the oil

5. Cook for 20 minutes, rotate wings using tongs after the first 10 minutes

6. Once fully cooked, remove from air fryer and place in a bowl then cover with the warm buffalo sauce and toss to evenly coat.

Nutritional Information: 117kcal | Fat: 11.8g | Carbs: 1g | Protein: 2.2g

Breakfast Sandwich

Preparation Time: 10 minutes

Cook Time: 5 minutes

Servings: 1

Ingredients

- 1 slice English Bacon
- 1 slice bread
- 1 whole egg, cracked
- 1/2 cup butter
- Salt and pepper to taste

Procedures

1. Preheat Air Fryer to 300F.

2. Spread the butter on one side of the bread slice, add the cracked egg on top and season with the salt and pepper.

3. Place the Bacon n top and arrange the bread slice in the Air Fryer basket then cook for 4- 5 minutes.

Serve!

Nutritional Information: 320kcal | Fat: 13g | Carbs: 33g | Protein: 17g

Spicy Bacon

Preparation Time: 2 minutes

Cook Time: 12 minutes

Servings: 5

Ingredients

- 5 Slices bacon (thick cut)

Procedures

1. Arranged the Slices into the Air Fryer side by side

2. Cook at 390 degrees for 10 - 12 minutes (Cook time varies depending on how crispy you like your bacon)

3. Place on a napkin to absorb any excess grease

Repeat process for remaining Slices

Serve!

Fried Parmesan Zucchini

Preparation Time: 10 minutes

Cook Time: 32 minutes

Servings: 4

Ingredients

- 1/2 Cup parmesan cheese, grated
- 2 Medium Zucchini
- 1/2 Teaspoon garlic powder
- 1/4 Almond flour
- 1 Teaspoon Italian seasoning
- 1 Large egg
- Avocado oil spray

Procedures

1. Slice the Zucchini into 1/4 to 1/3 of an inch slice.

2. Beat the egg in a bowl

3. Mix the Parmesan cheese, almond flour, Italian seasoning and garlic powder in a second bowl

4. Dip the Zucchini slice in the egg mixture first, then dip it in the parmesan cheese mixture.

5. Set it on the parchment air fryer tray. Repeat until the tray is full then lightly spray coated Zucchini with avocado oil spray.

6. Cook at 370F for 8 minutes

7. Remove tray and flip the zucchini then spray with the avocado oil and cook for another 8 minutes

8. Repeat for the other batch of Zucchini

Serve Warm!

Nutritional Information: 92kcal | Fat: 5g | Carbs: 5g | Protein: 6g

Herbed Tomatoes

Preparation Time: 5 minutes

Cook Time: 20 minutes

Servings: 2

Ingredients

- 1 Pound of cherry tomatoes cut into halves
- 1 Teaspoon cilantro, chopped
- 1 Teaspoon rosemary, chopped
- 1 Cucumber, chopped
- 1 Teaspoon oregano, chopped
- 1 Teaspoon Basil, chopped
- Olive oil to grease

- 1 Spring Onion, chopped
- Salt and black pepper to taste

Procedures

1. Grease Tomatoes with the oil, season with the salt and pepper and place in Air Fryer.

2. Cook for 20 minutes at 320F and then place in a bowl.

3. Toss the remaining ingredients in and serve!

Nutritional Information: 140kcal | Fat: 2g | Carbs: 8g | Protein: 4g

Spicy Bacon Bites

Preparation Time: 5 minutes

Cook Time: 5 minutes

Servings: 4

Ingredients

- 4 Strips of bacon
- 1/2 Cup of crushed pork rinds
- 1/4 Cup of hot sauce

Procedures

1. Cut the bacon slices to 6 piece and put inside a bowl

2. Add the hot sauce to the bowl and ensure both side of the bacon get sauce

3. Dip the pieces of the bacon into the pork rinds, coating both sides

4. Cook on 350F for 10 minutes

Note: After 7 minutes, check to ensure it is not burning

Nutritional Information: 120.7kcal | Fat: 8.7g | Carbs: 0g | Protein: 7.3g

Mac and Cheese

Preparation Time: 15 minutes

Cook Time: 10 minutes

Servings: 2

Ingredients

- 1 Cup cheddar cheese, grated
- 1 Tablespoon Parmesan cheese
- 1 cup Macaroni, cooked
- 1/2 Cup warm milk
- Salt and pepper to taste

Procedures

1. Preheat Air Fryer to 350F

2. Add the Macaroni to an ovenproof baking dish, stir in the cheddar and milk then season with the salt and pepper.

3. Place the dish in the Air Fryer and cook for 10 minutes.

4. Sprinkle with Parmesan Cheese once done

Serve!!

Nutritional Information: 375kcal | Fat: 1.8g | Carbs: 23g | Protein: 6.4g

Radish Hash Browns with Air Fryer

Preparation Time: 10 minutes

Cook Time: 13 minutes

Servings: 4

Ingredients

- 1 Teaspoon powdered Onion, granulated
- 1 Pound of washed Radishes
- 1 Tablespoon of Coconut Oil
- 1/4 Teaspoon of Freshly Ground Black Pepper
- 1 Medium of (Yellow/Brown) Onion
- 1/2 Teaspoon of Paprika
- 1 Teaspoon of powdered Garlic
- 3/4 Teaspoon of Sea Salt

Procedures

1. Cut off the roots of the Radishes and trim steams

2. Grate the Radishes and onions with a food processor

3. Place the Radishes and Onions into the Air Fryer basket and cook for 8 minutes at 360 degrees. Shake at intervals

4. Place the Radishes and onions in the Air Fryer and cook for 8 minutes at 360 degrees. Shake at intervals

5. Place the radishes and onions back into the bowl then add the seasonings and cook for 5 minutes at 400 degrees. Shaking after the first 3 minutes

Pan de Yuca (Colombian)

Preparation Time: 15 minutes

Cook Time: 15 minutes

Servings: 12

Ingredients

- 4 Oz of Tapioca Flour (With a little extra)
- 1.5 Teaspoons Baking Powder
- 10 Oz of Cheese
- 21 Grams of Heavy Cream
- 2 Large Eggs

Procedures

1. Process all the ingredients in a food processor until a ball is form

2. Sprinkle the extra Tapioca flour onto a bread board and turn out the dough.

3. Knead the dough until it is smooth and does not stick

4. Divide the dough into 12 even pieces and roll into 16 balls

5. Place in Air Fryer and cook for 8 minutes at 400 degrees.

6. Remove from Air Fryer and cool (preferably on a baker's rack) for 10 minutes

Enjoy

Nutritional Information: 135kcal | Fat: 8g | Carbs: 9g | Protein: 6g

Tomato and Eggs

Preparation Time: 5 minutes

Cook Time: 30 minutes

Servings: 2

Ingredients

- 2 Eggs
- 1/2 Cup of chopped tomatoes
- 2 Tablespoons of chopped red onion
- 1/2 Cup of shredded cheddar cheese
- 1/4 Cup milk
- Salt and black pepper to taste

Procedures

1. Mix all the ingredients in a bowl except the cheese and stir well

2. Put mixture in a pan and place in the Air Fryer.

3. Cook for 30 minutes at 350F

4. Divide and Serve.

Nutritional Information: 210kcal | Fat: 4g | Carbs: 12g | Protein: 0g

LUNCH RECIPES

Chicken Jalfrezi

Preparation Time: 10 minutes

Cook Time: 15 minutes

Servings: 4

Ingredients

- 1 Pound Boneless Skinless Chicken Thighs cut into large, 2-inch pieces
- 1/2-1 teaspoon cayenne
- 1 Cup Chopped Onion
- 1 Teaspoon Garam Masala
- 2 Cups chopped bell pepper
- 1 Teaspoon Turmeric
- 2 Tablespoons oil
- 1 Teaspoon Salt

- For the Sauce
- 1 Teaspoon Garam Masala
- 1/4 Cup tomato sauce
- 1/2 Teaspoon cayenne
- 1/2 Teaspoon Salt
- 1 Tablespoon water

Procedures

1. Mix the Chicken, peppers, onions, oil, salt, gram masala, turmeric and cayenne in a large bowl

2. Place the chicken and vegetables in the Air Fryer Basket.

3. Cook for 15 minutes for 360F, stir and toss half way through.

Prepare Sauce alongside

1. In a small microwave bowl, combine the tomato sauce, garam masala, salt, water and cayenne.

2. Microwave for 2 minutes. Remove and stir halfway through.

3. Once the chicken is cooked, place the chicken and vegetables in a large bowl.

4. Pour the sauce over them and toss to cover the chicken and vegetables evenly with the sauce.

Serve with rice or a side salad.

Nutritional Information: 247kcal | Fat: 12g | Carbs: 9g | Protein: 23g

Cilantro Pesto Chicken Legs

Preparation Time: 10 minutes

Cook Time: 20 minutes

Servings: 2

Ingredients

- 8 Cloves Garlic
- 4 Chicken drumsticks
- 2 Tablespoons lemon juice
- 1/2 Cup cilantro
- 1/2 Jalapeño pepper
- 1 Teaspoon Salt
- 2 Thin slices ginger
- 2 Tablespoons oil

Procedures

1. Place the chicken drumsticks on a flat tray and use the tip of a sharp knife to score small slashes into the chicken at regular intervals to ensure it marinates thoroughly

2. Chop finely the Pepper, garlic, ginger and cilantro and place in a small bowl.

3. Add salt, lemon juice and oil to the chopped vegetables and mix well.

4. Spread the mixture over the chicken and massage the marinade into the chicken.

5. Allow the chicken to marinate for 30 minutes or up to 24 hours in the refrigerator.

6. When ready to cook, place the chicken legs into the Air Fryer basket, skin side up.

7. Cook for 20 minutes at 390F, flip halfway through.

8. Remove and serve with a lot of napkins.

Mascarpone Mushroom Pasta

Preparation Time: 10 minutes

Cook Time: 15 minutes

Servings: 4

Ingredients

- 8 Ounces of diced Mascarpone Cheese
- 4 Cups sliced mushrooms
- 1 Cup Chopped Onion
- 2 Teaspoons Minced Garlic
- 1/2 Cup shredded Parmesan cheese
- 1/4 Cup Cream
- 1/2 Teaspoon Red Pepper Flakes
- 1 Teaspoon Salt
- 1 Teaspoon Dried Thyme
- 1 Teaspoon Ground Black Pepper

Procedures

1. Grease a 7x3 inch pan and set aside.

2. Get a medium bowl, combine the garlic, cheese, cream, pepper, red pepper flakes, mushrooms onion, salt and thyme and pour into the greased pan.

3. Cook for 15 minutes at 350F. Stir halfway through.

4. Meanwhile, boil 4 cups of pasta and divide across four bowls

5. Remove the mushrooms and mascarpone mixture and divide evenly on the pasta.

6. Sprinkle the parmesan cheese and serve

Nutritional Information: 402kcal | Fat: 35g | Carbs: 10g | Protein: 12g

Korean Chicken Wings

Preparation Time: 10 minutes

Cook Time: 30 minutes

Servings: 4

Ingredients

For the Wings:

- 2 Pounds chicken wings
- 1 Teaspoon Ground Black Pepper
- 1 Teaspoon Salt

For the Sauce:

- 1 Tablespoon minced ginger

- 2 Tablespoons gochujang
- 2 Packets Splenda or sugar
- 1 Tablespoon mayonnaise
- 1 Teaspoon agave nectar
- 1 Tablespoon Minced Garlic
- 1 Tablespoon Sesame Oil

For Finishing(optional):

- 2 Teaspoons Sesame Seeds
- 1/4 Cup chopped green onions

Procedures

1. Preheat Air Fryer to 400F

2. Get a small roasting pan (or baking pan) and line it with foil. Place a rack inside this pan.

3. Salt and Pepper the chicken wings and place on the rack. You want to use a rack to raise them, so they can drip fat into the tray below.

4. Set the timer to 20 minutes and allow the chicken wings to cook, turning once at 10 minutes.

5. As the chicken bakes or air fries, mix together all the sauce ingredients and let the sauce marinate while the chicken wings finish cooking.

6. As you near the 20-minute mark use a thermometer to check the meat. When the chicken wings reach 160F remove them from the oven and place into a bowl.

7. Pour about half the sauce on the wings, and toss to coat the wings with the sauce.

Place the chicken wings back into the oven or air fryer and cook for another 5 minutes until the sauce has glazed over, and the chicken is completely cooked and has reached at least 165F.

8. Remove, sprinkle with sesame seeds and chopped green onions and serve with plenty of napkins.

Nutritional Information: 356kcal | Fat: 26g | Carbs: 6g | Protein: 23g

Spicy Pepper Scotch Eggs

Preparation Time: 20 minutes
Cook Time: 25 minutes

Servings: 4

Ingredients

- 2 Teaspoons coarse-ground mustard
- 1 Pound bulk pork sausage
- 4 Hard-cooked eggs peeled
- 1 Tablespoon finely chopped fresh chives
- 2 Tablespoons finely chopped fresh parsley
- 1 Cup shredded Parmesan cheese
- 1/8 Teaspoon freshly grated nutmeg
- 1/8 Teaspoon Salt
- 1/8 Teaspoon Ground Black Pepper

Procedures

1. Get a large bowl and mix the sausage, parsley, nutmeg, mustard, salt and black pepper until everything is properly combined then shape the mixture into four patties of equal size

2. Put each egg on a sausage patty and shape the sausage around the egg then dip each in the shredded parmesan cheese to cover completely, pressing lightly to adhere making sure the shreds are well pressed into the meat so that it does not fly around the Air Fryer.

3. Arrange the eggs in Air Fryer basket. Spray lightly with nonstick vegetable oil.

4. Cook for 15 minutes at 400F

Serve with coarse-ground mustard

Fried Cheesecake Bites

Preparation Time: 60 minutes

Cook Time: 3 minutes

Servings: 16

Ingredients

- 1/2 Cup erythritol
- 2 Tablespoons erythritol
- 8 Ounces cream cheese
- 1/2 teaspoon vanilla extract
- 4 Tablespoons heavy cream, divided
- 1/2 cup almond flour

Procedures

1. Sit the cheese on the counter for 20 minutes to soften

2. Fit a stand mixer with paddle attachment

3. Mix the already softened cheese, vanilla, 1/2 cup erythritol and heavy cream until smooth.

4. Scoop onto a parchment paper lined baking sheet.

5. Freeze for 30 minutes until it is firm

6. Mix the Almond flour with the 2 Tablespoons erythritol in a small bowl.

7. Dip the frozen cheesecake bites into the 2 Tablespoon cream then roll into the almond flour mixture.

8. Cook in Air Fryer for 2 minutes

Serve!!

Nutritional Information: 80kcal | Fat: 3g | Carbs: 2g | Protein: 2g

Steak Nuggets with a white barbecue sauce

Preparation Time: 10 minutes

Cook Time: 40 minutes

Servings: 4

Ingredients

Steak Nuggets:

- 1 lb. steak, cut into chunks
- 1 Cup grated parmesan cheese
- 1 Cup pork panko crumbs
- 2 Eggs
- 1 Teaspoon seasoned salt

White Barbecue Sauce:

- 2 Teaspoon horseradish sauce
- 1 tablespoon spicy brown mustard
- 1 Cup mayo
- 1/4 Teaspoon garlic powder
- 1/4 Cup white vinegar
- 1/2 Teaspoon black pepper
- 1/4 Teaspoon paprika
- 1/2 Teaspoon salt

Procedures

1. Combine the pork panko, parmesan cheese and seasoned salt in a bowl.

2. Beat 2 Eggs in another bowl.

3. Dip chunks of steak into the Eggs, then breading. Repeat this step again

4. Freeze breaded steak with a freezer safe plate for 30 minutes before frying

5. While waiting, whisk all the barbecue sauce ingredients together in a bowl, until smooth. Keep refrigerated until ready to serve.

Vietnamese Grilled Pork Thit Nuong

Preparation Time: 40 minutes

Cook Time: 10 minutes

Servings: 4

Ingredients

For the Marinade

- 2 Tablespoons of oil
- 2 Tablespoon of sugar
- 1 Tablespoon of Garlic, minced
- 2 Teaspoons of dark soy sauce
- 1 Tablespoon of Fish Sauce
- 1 Tablespoon of lemongrass paste, minced
- 1/2 Teaspoon of Ground Black Pepper
- 1/4 Cup of minced onions
- 1 Pound of pork shoulder (thinly sliced into 1/2 in slices)

For Finishing

- 2 Tablespoons of chopped parsley
- 1/4 cup of crushed roasted peanuts

Procedures

1. Whisk the onions, soy sauce, oil, garlic, lemon grass, fish sauce, sugar and pepper

2. Cut the slices of the pork shoulder into 4-inch pieces

3. Add the Pork to the mixture and allow to rest for half an hour to 24 hours.

4. Remove the pork from the marinade and place the slices in a single layer in the Air Fryer basket

5. Cook at 400F for 10 minutes. Flip halfway through.

Serve with the parsley and roasted peanut sprinkled on top.

Nutritional Information: 231kcal | Fat: 16g | Carbs: 4g | Protein: 16g

Spicy Jicama Fries

Preparation Time: 30 minutes

Cook Time: 20 minutes

Servings: 4

Ingredients

- 1 Jicama
- 2 Teaspoon garlic powder
- 2 1/2 Teaspoon paprika
- 2 Tablespoon olive oil
- 2 Teaspoon salt
- 1 1/4 Teaspoon dried thyme

- 1 1/4 Teaspoon dried oregano
- 1 Teaspoon black pepper
- 1 Teaspoon onion powder
- 1 Teaspoon cayenne pepper
- 1/2 Teaspoon red pepper flakes (optional)

Procedures

1. Peel and slice the Jicama into thin fries.

2. Add the Jicama in a boiling water and boil for 20 minutes or until it is no longer crunchy.

3. Remove and pat dry then place in a large bowl.

4. Add the rest of the ingredients to the bowl and mix well.

5. Place the fries in a single layer in the Air Fryer Basket then cook at 400F for 20 minutes flipping halfway through.

Garlic Butter Naan Bread

Preparation Time: 10 minutes

Cook Time: 8 minutes

Servings: 4

Ingredients

Bread:

- 2 Cups boiling water
- 2 Tablespoon ground psyllium husk powder
- 1 Cup coconut flour
- 1/3 Cup coconut oil, melted
- 1/2 Teaspoon baking powder
- 1 Egg

- 1/2 Teaspoon onion powder
- 1 Teaspoon salt
- Sea salt

Garlic Butter:

- 4 Oz butter
- Pinch of parsley
- 2 Garlic cloves, minced

Procedures

1. Combine the egg, baking powder, coconut flour, onion powder and salt in a bowl, add coconut oil and boiling water then mix thoroughly.

2. Leave for five minutes to allow dough rise. If it is too firm, add in boiling water, if it is runny, add more psyllium husk powder.

3. Divide the dough into 5-8 pieces and form into balls. Flatten with your hand on parchment paper.

4. Put inside the Air Fryer basket on perforated parchment paper and spread coconut oil on the top of each piece.

5. Cook at 400F for 8 minutes.

6. While waiting, melt the butter and stir in the garlic and parsley.

7. Once the bread is done, brush the garlic butter mixture on top each piece, pour the remaining of the garlic butter mixture in a bowl and use it to dip the pieces of bread in as desired.

Buffalo Cauliflower

Preparation Time: 10 minutes

Cook Time: 20 minutes

Servings: 2

Ingredients

- 1 Large cauliflower head
- 1/2 Teaspoon of Worcestershire sauce
- 1/4 Cup of coconut oil
- 1 Tablespoon of smoked paprika
- 2 Teaspoons of apple cider vinegar
- 1/2 Teaspoon of cayenne pepper
- 1/8 Teaspoon of powdered garlic
- 3/4 Cup of hot sauce
- 1/2 Teaspoon of salt
- 1/8 Teaspoon of powdered onion

Procedures

1. Cut the Cauliflowers into small and medium sizes of florets

2. Combine the rest of the ingredients and mix!

3. Toss the Cauliflower with the sauce and let it sit for 10 minutes to enable the sauce to seep into the cauliflower

4. Put half of the Cauliflower into the air fryer basket and cook to 310F for 10 minutes

5. Shake the Air fryer basket after the first 5 minutes to toss the florets and then continue cooking

6. Remove from heat and repeat the process for the other half of the Cauliflower

Serve with Blue cheese dressing or ranch

Brazilian Chicken

Preparation Time: 5 minutes

Cook Time: 25 minutes

Servings: 4

Ingredients

- 1.5 pounds chicken drumsticks
- 2 tablespoons of oil
- 1 teaspoon cumin seeds
- 1/2 teaspoon of Cayenne
- 1 teaspoon Dried Oregano
- 1 teaspoon Turmeric
- 1 teaspoon of Dried Parsley
- 1/2 teaspoon Whole Black Peppercorns
- 1 teaspoon Salt
- 1/2 teaspoon of Coriander Seeds
- 1/4 cup of lime juice

Procedures

1. Blend the oregano, salt, turmeric, cumin, coriander seeds, cayenne pepper and peppercorns in a coffee grinder

2. Combine the lemon juice with the spices and oil in a medium bowl

3. Add the chicken to the mixture and stir until it is well coated with the marinade

4. Put the chicken in the fridge and allow to marinade for at least half a hour to whenever you are ready to cook.

5. Place the chicken in the air fryer basket, skin side up

6. Cook at 390F for 20 - 25 minutes. Flip halfway through.

Serve with plenty of napkins

Nutritional Information: 253kcal | Fat: 17g | Carbs: 2g | Protein: 20g

Tomato Basil Scallops

Preparation Time: 5 minutes

Cook Time: 10 minutes

Servings: 2

Ingredients

- 8 Jumbo sea scallops
- 3/4 Cup of heavy whipping cream
- 1 12 Oz package frozen spinach (thawed and drained)
- 1 Tablespoon of Tomato Paste
- 1 Tablespoon of chopped fresh basil
- 1 Teaspoon Garlic, Minced
- 1/2 Teaspoon of Salt
- 1/2 Teaspoon of Ground Black Pepper

- Cooking Oil Spray
- Extra salt and pepper to season scallops

Procedures

1. Put the spinach in an even layer in a 7-inch heatproof pan. Spray pan before use

2. Spray the Scallop on both sides with vegetable oil, sprinkle little salt and pepper on them then put in the pan on top of the spinach

3. Mix the cream, basil, salt, tomato paste, garlic and pepper in a small bowl and pour over the scallop and spinach.

4. Cook for 10 minutes at 350F.

Serve immediately

Nutritional Information: 359kcal | Fat: 33g | Carbs: 6g | Protein: 9g

Cauliflower Rice

Preparation Time: 10 minutes

Cook Time: 20 minutes

Servings: 3

Ingredients

CLASS 1

- 1/2 Cup of onion, diced
- 1/2 Block of firm or extra firm tofu
- 1 Teaspoon of turmeric
- 1 Cup of carrot, diced - about 1 to 2 carrots
- 2 Tablespoons of reduced sodium soy sauce

CLASS 2

- 1/2 Cup frozen peas
- 3 Cups of riced Cauliflower
- 1 Tablespoon of rice vinegar
- 2 Cloves of garlic - minced
- 1 (1/2) Teaspoons of toasted sesame oil
- 1/2 Cup of finely chopped broccoli
- 1 Tablespoon of ginger, minced

Procedures

1. Crumble the Tofu in a large bowl with all the ingredients in CLASS 1. Air fry at 370F for 10 minutes

2. While cooking, combine all the CLASS 2 ingredients in a large bowl

3. After cooking for 10 minutes, (in step 1) add the CLASS 2 ingredients to the Air Fryer, shake gently fry for another 10 minutes at the same temperature, shaking after the first 5 minutes

4. You can cook for additional 3-6 minutes if it does not look done enough to your liking, ensure you shake and check in every couple of minutes.

Honey roasted carrots

Preparation time: 5 minutes

Cook Time: 12 minutes

Serving: 4

Ingredients

- 1 Tablespoon of Honey
- Carrots cut into large chunks
- Salt and pepper to taste
- 1 Tablespoon of Olive oil

Procedures

1. Mix the carrots with the honey and olive oil ensuring the carrots are well covered

2. Season with the salt and pepper then cook in Air Fryer at 200 degrees for 12 minutes

Serve Hot!

Chicken Parmesan

Preparation Time: 15 minutes

Cook Time: 10 minutes

Servings: 6

Ingredients

- 4 Chicken breasts (skinless and thinly sliced)
- 3 Eggs beaten
- 1 Jar of Marinara Sauce

- 1 Cup of Panko bread crumbs
- 1/2 Cup of mozzarella cheese shredded
- 1/2 Cup of parmesan cheese grated
- Salt and pepper to taste
- Olive oil cooking spray
- 3/4 Cup of marinara sauce
- Spaghetti as desired

Procedures

1. Preheat the Air Fryer to 460 and spray basket with cooking spray

2. Put Chicken on a hard surface

3. Mix the Bread crumbs, parmesan and seasonings in a large bowl. Stir!!

4. Place the eggs in a bowl and beat until frothy

5. First dip the chicken in the egg and then in the bread crumbs mixture

6. Place chicken in Air Fryer and spray the top of the chicken with the olive oil then cook for 7 minutes.

7. Put the chicken on a baking sheet and set your oven temperature to broil on high

8. Top each of the chicken with marinara sauce and the mozzarella

9. Cook for 3 minutes

10. Cook your spaghetti as desired

11. Once cooked, toss the Pasta in the leftover marinara.

Place the chicken on top of the pasta and Serve!!

Indian Kheema Meatloaf

Preparation Time: 10 minutes

Cook Time: 18 minutes

Servings: 4

Ingredients

- 1 lb. Lean Ground Beef
- 1 Cup onion diced
- 2 Teaspoon of Garam Masala
- 2 Eggs
- 1/8 Teaspoon of Ground Cardamom
- 1 Teaspoon of cayenne
- 1/4 Cup of chopped cilantro
- 1 Teaspoon of Turmeric
- 1/2 Teaspoon ground cinnamon
- 1 Tablespoon of minced ginger
- 1 Tablespoon of Minced Garlic
- 1 Teaspoon of Salt

Procedures

1. Mix thoroughly but gently all ingredients in a large bowl until properly mixed

2. Put the seasoned meat into a heat-safe 8-inch round pan.

3. Cook for 15 minutes at 360F. Use a meat thermometer to ensure the meatloaf reached an internal temperature of 160F

4. Remove the pan and drain excess fat then slice the beef into 4 pieces.

Serve

Nutritional Information: 260kcal | Fat: 13g | Carbs: 6g | Protein: 26g

Indian Spicy Fennel Chicken

Preparation Time: 10 minutes

Cook Time: 15 minutes

Servings: 4

Ingredients

For the Chicken Fry

- 1 Teaspoons of ground fennel seeds
- 1 Pound of Chicken Thighs (Boneless Skinless) each thigh cut into 3 pieces
- 2 Teaspoons Minced Garlic
- 1/2 -1 Teaspoon Cayenne
- 1 Large onion cut into 1.5-inch-thick slices
- 1 Tablespoon of Coconut Oil
- 2 Teaspoons minced ginger
- 1 Teaspoon of Turmeric
- 1 Teaspoons of Garam Masala
- 1 Teaspoons Smoked Paprika
- 1 Teaspoon Salt
- Vegetable Oil to spray the chicken while cooking

For Finishing

- 1/4 cup Chopped Cilantro
- 2 teaspoons fresh lemon juice

Procedures

1. Use a fork to pierce the chicken all over in order for the marinade to penetrate

2. Mix all the ingredients for the Chicken fry in a large bowl and allow the chicken to marinade for 30 minutes or 24 hours

3.Put the Chicken and vegetables inside the Air Fryer basket and spray the chicken and onion with vegetable oil.

4. Cook for 15 minutes at 360F, spraying the chicken with more oil and shaking about halfway through.

5. Ensure the chicken has reached an internal temperature of 165 using a meat thermometer.

6. Garnish with the Lemon juice and cilantro

Nutritional Information: 190kcal | Fat: 8g | Carbs: 5g | Protein: 22g

Salmon Bok Choy

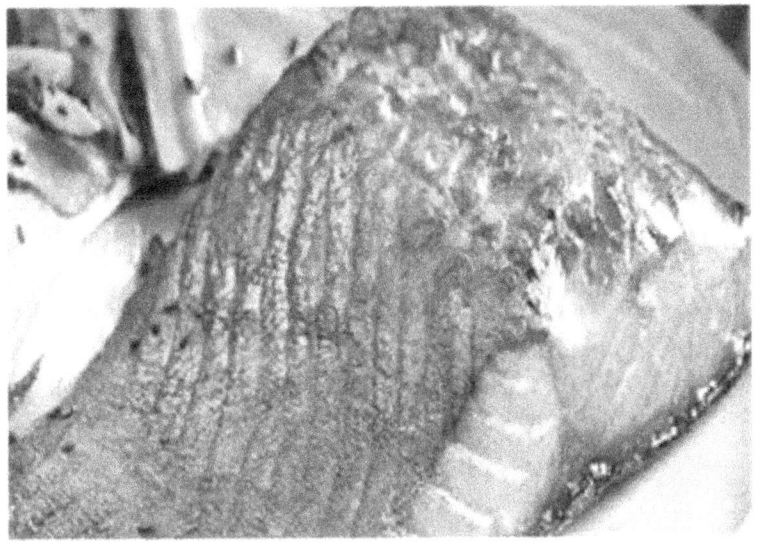

Preparation Time: 20 minutes

Cook Time: 12 minutes

Servings: 2

Ingredients

- 2 5-Ounce Salmon fillets
- 3 Tablespoons of Rice Vinegar
- 2 Minced Garlic Cloves
- 2 Teaspoons finely grated orange zest
- 1 Tablespoon of fresh ginger, minced
- 1 Tablespoon of Vegetable Oil
- 1/2 Cup of fresh Orange juice
- 1/2 Teaspoon Salt
- 1/4 cup of Soy Sauce
- For the Vegetables
- 1/2 Teaspoon Sesame Seeds, toasted
- 1 Tablespoon of Dark Sesame Oil
- 2 Heads of baby bok choy halved lengthwise

- 2 Ounces shiitake mushrooms stemmed (stems discarded)
- Salt to taste

Procedures

For the fish

1. In a small bowl, whisk together soy sauce, garlic, orange zest and juice, vinegar, ginger, vegetable oil and salt. Reserve half of the marinade.

2. Place the Salmon in a resealable bag the size of a gallon and pour the other half of the marinade over the Salmon then seal and massage to coat.

3. Allow to marinate for half an hour at room temperature

4. Place the Salmon in the Air Fryer and cook for 12 minutes at 400F.

For the Vegetables

1. Brush Bok choy and mushroom caps all over with Sesame oil and season lightly with salt.

2. Once the Salmon has cooked for 6 minutes, add the vegetables around the Salmon in the Air Fryer Basket and continue cooking.

Serve with some of the reserved marinade drizzled on it and sprinkle vegetables with sesame seeds.

Nutritional Information: 195kcal | Fat: 14g | Carbs: 12g | Protein: 4g

Fried Pickles

Preparation Time: 10 minutes

Cook Time: 10 minutes

Servings: 4

Ingredients

- 1/4 Cup of freshly grated parmesan
- 3/4 Cup of breadcrumbs
- 2 Cup of dill pickle slices
- 1 Egg, whisked with 1 tablespoon water
- 1 Teaspoon of powdered garlic
- Ranch, for serving
- 1 Teaspoon of dried oregano

Procedures

1. Pat the Pickle chips dry using paper towels.

2. Stir the breadcrumbs, parmesan, oregano and Garlic Powdered in a bowl

3. Dredge the Pickle chip in the egg then in the breadcrumb mixture.

4. Place in the air fryer and cook for 10 minutes at highest temperature.

Serve immediately, with Ranch for dipping.

Cornish hen

Preparation Time: 5 mins

Cook Time: 25 mins

Servings: 2

Ingredients

- 1 Cornish hen
- Olive oil spray (Or Coconut Spray)
- Paprika
- Salt
- Black pepper

Procedures

1. Mix all Spices together

2. Rub the Hen with the spices

3. Spray Air Fryer Basket with Olive oil spray

4. Place the hen in the Air Fryer and cook at 390F for 25 minutes. Flip after the first 13 minutes

Carefully remove and Serve!

Hot Dogs

Preparation Time: 10 minutes

Cook Time: 8 minutes

Servings: 4

Ingredient

- 4 Hot dogs all beef

Procedures

1. Give the Hot Dogs three small, shallow and perpendicular cuts down the middle (known as Scoring) so they have little slits and will prevent it from bursting

2. Place in Air Fryer and cook at 375F for 5 minutes

3. Flip side and cook for additional 3 minutes

Remove once done and Serve as desired!

Southern Fried Catfish

Preparation Time: 15 minutes

Cook Time: 13 minutes

Servings: 4

Ingredients

- 1/2 Cup of Yellow Mustard
- 2 Pounds Catfish Fillets
- 1 Lemon
- 1 Cup of Milk

For the Seasoning

- 1/2 Cup of Cornmeal
- 1/4 Teaspoon of powdered Onion
- 1/4 Teaspoon of Chili Powder
- 2 Tablespoons of Dried Parsley Flakes
- 1/4 Cup of Flour
- 1/4 Teaspoon of powdered Garlic
- 1/2 Teaspoon of Salt
- 1/4 Teaspoon of Freshly Ground Black Pepper
- 1/4 Teaspoon Cayenne Pepper

Procedures

1. Place the catfish in a flat container and add the milk.

2. Cut the lemon into half and squeeze 2 teaspoons of juice into the milk to produce buttermilk

3. Place the container in Fridge and allow the fillets soak for 15 minutes

4. Combine all the seasoning ingredients in a shallow bowl

5. Remove the fillets and pat them dry with a paper towel

6. Spread the Mustard lavishly on both sides of the fillets

7. Dip each of the fillet into the SEASONING ingredients mixture and coat well to make a thick coating

8. Grease Air Fryer Basket and place the Fillets inside, Spray generously with oil

9. Cook at 390 degree for 10 minutes.

10. Once 10 minutes is expired, flip over the fillets, spray with oil and cook for additional 3 to 5 minutes

Tijuana Street Taco

Preparation Time: 13 minutes

Cook Time: 8 minutes

Servings: 10

Ingredients

- 10 Fresh Corn Tortillas
- 1 Teaspoon of Chipotle Peppers in Adobo
- 1.5 Teaspoons of Ground Cumin
- 1 Fresh Lime cut into wedges

- 1.5 Teaspoons of Dried Oregano
- 1.5 Teaspoon of Ground Achiote (Annato Seed)
- 2 Pounds of Flap Meat (Flap Steak)
- 4 cloves of Fresh Garlic, minced
- 2 Tablespoons of Dark Brown Sugar, divided
- 2 teaspoons of Salt
- 1 Can Pineapple Slices
- Homemade Pico de Gallo

Procedures

1. Put the sliced meat into a medium bowl then add the chipotle, Adobo sauce, oregano, cumin, Achiote, 1/4 cup of pineapple juice, 1 tbsp of brown sugar and salt. Cover and put in the fridge for about 1 hour

2. Preheat the Air Fryer at 400 degrees for 5 minutes then grease the Air Fryer basket with oil lightly

3. Place the meat in the Air Fryer Basket and cover with the Pineapple rings, sprinkle the pineapple with the remaining 1 tbsp of brown sugar then cook for 8 minutes at 390F

Serve in warm corn/ flour Tortillas with Pico de Gallo and a lime wedge.

Enjoy pineapple on the side

Nutritional Information: 154kcal | Fat: 6g | Carbs: 3g | Protein: 19g

Chicken Without Gluten

Preparation Time: 5 minutes

Cook Time: 30 minutes

Servings: 8

Ingredients

- 16 Chicken Pieces (preferably skin on)
- 1/2 Table spoon of Paprika
- 2 Teaspoons of Seasoning
- 3/4 Cup of Almond Flour
- 1 Teaspoon of Powdered Garlic
- 1 Teaspoon of Black Pepper
- Salt, as desired preferably 1-2 teaspoon.

Procedures

1. Mix all ingredients except the chicken in a large Ziploc bag.

2. Add 4 pieces of chicken to the bag and seal the top.

3. Coat the chicken by shaking the bag.

4. Transfer to the air fryer.

5. Arrange the chicken in a single layer.

6. Repeat the procedures with the remaining pieces of chicken.

7. Cook for 30 minutes at 370 degrees and flip the chicken after the first 15 minutes

8. Immediately serve

Nutritional Information: 540kcal | Fat: 27g | Carbs: 2g | Protein: 66g

Steak Bites

Preparation Time: 10 mins

Cook Time: 20 mins

Servings: 4

Ingredients

- 1 lb. steaks
- 1/2 lb. potatoes
- 1/2 Teaspoon of powdered garlic
- 2 Tablespoons melted butter, (or oil)
- Salt, to taste
- 1 Teaspoon of Worcestershire sauce
- Black pepper, to taste
- Minced parsley, garnish

Optional:

- Melted butter
- Chili Flakes

Procedures

1. Cut the Potatoes into 1.2"pieces. Cut the Steaks into 1/2"cubes and patted dry

2. Add the Potatoes to an already heated pot of water and cook for 5 minutes (or until soft as desired) and then drain

3. Combine the steak cubes and potatoes. Coat with the butter then season with the sauce, garlic, salt and pepper

4. Preheat the Air Fryer at 400F for 4 minutes.

5. Place the steak and potatoes in even layer in the Air Fryer basket then fry at 400F for 10 - 18 minutes.

Note: Flip and shake the steak and potatoes about 3 times through the cooking process. Cooking time depends on your preference of doness, thickness of the steak and size of the Air Fryer

6. Once it reaches your preferred doneness, remove!

7. Garnish with parsley and season with the optional ingredients above. You can season with additional peer and salt as desired.

Serve warm

DINNER RECIPES

Blue Cheese Ribeye Steak

Preparation Time: 15 minutes

Cook Time: 7 minutes

Servings: 2

Ingredients

- 2 (12 - 16) Ounce Rib Eye Steaks
- 2 Teaspoons of Salt
- 1.5 Teaspoon of Freshly Ground Black Pepper
- 1 Teaspoon of powdered Garlic
- 2 Tablespoons of Blue Cheese Butter

Procedures

1. Remove the Butter from the fridge 20 minutes before starting the procedures

2. Follow directions to prepare the Butter

3. Preheat the Air fryer at 400 degrees for 15 minutes

4. Coat the Steaks on both sides with the salt, pepper and garlic powder

5. Put the steaks in the Air fryer and cook for 7 minutes at 400 degrees. Flipping halfway through

6. Let cool for 2 minutes then top with the cheese butter

Nutritional Information: 829kcal | Fat: 60g | Carbs: 2g | Protein: 69g

Buffalo Chicken Legs

Preparation time: 5 minutes

Cook time: 25 minutes

Servings: 4

Ingredients

- 1/4 Cup of Sauce
- 2 lbs. skinless Chicken Drumsticks
- 2 Tablespoons of melted Ghee

Procedures

1. Pre heat Air Fryer at 400F for 2-minute after spraying basket with nonstick oil

2. Put the drumsticks in basket and fry for 20 minutes at same temperature, flipping the drumsticks after the first 15 minutes

3. Mix the ghee and hot sauce in a wide bowl and add the drumsticks then toss in sauce.

4. Return the drumstick to Basket and spoon the remaining sauce over the top of the drumsticks

5. Air fry for 5 minutes.

Serve with Whole 30 ranch dip, carrots and celery

Nutritional Information: 983kcal | Fat: 29g | Carbs: 5g | Protein: 110g

Zesty Ranch Air Fryer Fish Fillets

Preparation Time: 5 minutes

Cook Time: 12 minutes

Servings: 4

Ingredients

- 2 Eggs beaten
- 3/4 Cup bread crumbs
- 1 30g Packet dry ranch-style dressing mix
- Lemon wedges to garnish
- 4 Tilapia salmon or preferred fish fillets
- 2 (1/2) Tablespoons of vegetable oil

Procedures

1. Preheat Air Fryer to 180C

2. Mix the breadcrumbs and the ranch dressing mix together

3. Add the oil to the mixture and keep stirring until it becomes loose and crumbly

4. Dip the fish fillets into the egg and let the excess drip off then dip into the crumb mixture and ensure the fish fillet is coated evenly and thoroughly

5. Carefully place it into the Air Fryer and cook for 12 minutes (Cooking time varies depending on the thickness of the fillets)

Serve once done! Garnish with the lemon wedges as desired

Nutritional Information: 315kcal | Fat: 14g | Carbs: 8g | Protein: 38g

Crispy Pork Belly

Preparation Time: 10 mins

Cook Time: 30 mins

Servings: 4

Ingredients

- 2 Tablespoon of soy sauce
- 1 Pound of pork belly
- 1 Teaspoon salt
- 6 Cloves garlic
- 2 Bay leaves
- 1 Tablespoon of pepper

Procedures

1. Cut the pork into 3 thick chunks

2. Place all the ingredients into a pressure cooker and cook at high pressure for 15 minutes

3. Allow pot rests for 10 minutes then release all remaining pressure

4. Carefully remove meat from the pressure cooker and allow to dry and drain for 10 minutes.

5. Cut each of the 3 chunks of pork into 2 long slices and place in the air fryer

6. Set Air Fryer to 400o F and heat until the fat on the pork belly has crisped up, about 15 minutes

Serve!

Nutritional Information: 594kcal | Fat: 60g | Carbs: 0g | Protein: 11g

Turkey Breast Tenderloin

Preparation Time: 5 minutes

Cook Time: 25 minutes

Servings: 2

Ingredients

- 1 Turkey breast tenderloin
- 1/2 Teaspoon paprika
- 1/2 Teaspoon of sage
- 1/2 Teaspoon of thyme
- 1/2 Teaspoon of black pepper
- 1/2 Teaspoon of pink salt

Procedures

1. Mix all spices and herbs together.

2. Rub the turkey in the mixture

3. Spray Air Fryer basket with oil spray and Cook turkey at 350F for 25 minutes. Flip halfway through

Serve!!

Smoked BBQ Ribs

Preparation time: 35 minutes

Cook time: 30 minutes

Servings: 4

Ingredients

- 1/2 Cup BBQ sauce
- 2-3 Tablespoons of pork rub
- 1 Rack ribs (baby back or spare ribs)
- 1 Tablespoon of liquid smoke
- Salt and pepper to taste

Procedures

1. Remove the membrane from the back of the ribs. (It peels right off sometimes)

2. Cut the Ribs into halves and drizzle the smoke over the sides of the ribs, then season the sides of the ribs with the pork rub, salt and pepper

3. Cover the ribs and leave to rest at room temperature for 30 minutes

4. Place the ribs in the Air Fryer and cook at 360 degrees for 15 minutes

5. Remove and drizzle with the BBQ sauce.

Nutritional Information: 375kcal | Fat: 27g | Carbs: 12g | Protein: 18g

Brussels Sprouts

Preparation Time: 2 minutes

Cook Time: 10 minutes

Servings: 4

Ingredients

- 2 Cups of halved Brussels sprouts (sliced in half or thirds)
- 1 Tablespoon of vinegar
- 1 Tablespoon of olive oil
- 1/4 Teaspoon salt

Procedures

1. Toss the Brussels, vinegar, oil and salt in a bowl

2. Cook for 8-10 minutes at 400 degrees. Remove and shake after 5 minutes

Garlic Parmesan Breaded Fried Chicken Wings

Preparation Time: 10 minutes

Cook Time: 20 minutes

Servings: 4

Ingredients

- 16 Chicken wings drumettes
- 1/4 Cup of grated parmesan
- Cooking spray of choice
- 2 Tablespoon of (low-sodium) soy sauce
- 1 Teaspoon of powdered garlic
- 1 Teaspoon of parmesan
- 1/4 Cup of low-fat buttermilk
- 1/2 Cup of flour
- Seasoning to taste
- Pepper to taste

Procedures

1. Wash the chicken then pat dry and drizzle the soy sauce over the chicken.

2. Season chicken with the seasonings and place in a Ziploc bag then in a fridge for 30 minutes to marinate.

3. Once the chicken is marinated, add the parmesan and flour to another Ziploc bag

4. Put the buttermilk in a large bowl that can take in the chicken then coat each of the chicken with the buttermilk and put it in the bag with the flour. Shake to coat

5. Grease the air fryer basket with oil.

6. Use tongs to remove the chicken from the bag and arrange in the air fryer basket.

7. Spray the chicken with cooking spray and cook for 20 minutes at 400 degrees. Remove and shake the basket after every 5 minutes to ensure all the chicken are fully cooked

8. Garnish with the leftover Parmesan before serving

Fried Chicken

Preparation Time: 10 minutes

Cook Time: 20 minutes

Servings: 6

Ingredients

- 2 1/2 lbs. Chicken drumsticks
- 1/4 Teaspoon of Dried thyme
- 2 Large Eggs
- 1/4 Teaspoon of Black pepper
- 1 Teaspoon of Smoked paprika
- 1 Cup of Pork rinds (2.25 oz)
- 1/4 Cup of Coconut flour

- 1/2 Teaspoon of Powdered Garlic
- 1/2 Teaspoon of Sea salt

Procedures

1. Stir the sea salt, black pepper and coconut flour in a bowl. Bowl 1

2. Whisk the eggs together in another bowl. Bowl 2

3. Mix the powdered garlic, thyme and pork rinds in another bowl. Bowl 3

4. Dredge the pieces of chicken in Bowl 1

5. Dip in Bowl 2. Shake off the excess

6. Press into Bowl 3

NB: For best results, Keep the mixture of Bowl 3 in another bowl and add little at a time to the bowl where you will be coating the chicken.

7. Heat Air Fryer at 400 degrees for 5 minutes.

8. Grease the Air fryer metal basket lightly.

9. In a single layer, neatly arrange the breaded chicken. Do not let them touch each other

10. Return basket to Air Fryer and cook for 20 minutes until internal temperature is 165 degrees.

11. Serve

Crispy Veggie Fries

Preparation Time: 10 minutes

Cook Time: 8 minutes

Servings: 4

Ingredients

- 2 Tablespoons of nutritional yeast flakes, divided
- 1 Cup of panko bread crumbs
- Salt and pepper
- 2 Tablespoons of desired vegan egg powder
- 1 Cup of Rice Flour
- Assorted Veggies of choice
- 2/3 Cup of Cold Water

Procedures

Cut the Veggies into bite size chunks or French fry shapes such as cauliflower, zucchini, sweet onions, green beans or squash

1. Place the rice flour in a shallow dish. MIXTURE 1

2. Whisk together the Vegan Egg powder, bread crumbs, 1tbsp of the nutritional yeast and little salt and pepper in another shallow dish. MIXTURE 2

3. Mix together the bread crumbs and the other 1 tbsp of the nutritional yeast with little salt and pepper. MIXTURE 3

4. One Veggie at a time, dip in MIXTURE 1, then MIXTURE 2, then MIXTURE 3, pressing to set coating. Make as many as you like

5. Grease lightly the Air Fryer basket and carefully place the Veggie fries in the basket, give them a quick mist of oil

6. Cook at 380F for 8 minutes until golden and crispy

Serve hot with a desired sauce

Monkey Bread

Preparation time: 7 minutes

Cook time: 7 minutes

Servings: 3

Ingredients

- 1/2 Teaspoon cinnamon
- 1 Cup of non-fat Greek yogurt
- 1 Cup of self-rising flour
- 1 Teaspoon of sugar

Procedures

1. Mix the Yogurt and flour until dough is form (Will appear Crumbly at first)

2. Make a Round ball out of the dough and cut into 4ths

3. Take a wedge and form a flattened circular disc.

4. Cut into 8 pieces like pizza, and roll each wedge into balls

5. Put the Cinnamon and sugar into a plastic Ziploc bag, then add the balls of dough. Seal and shake thoroughly to evenly coat them

6. Get a mini loaf pan and spray with nonstick spray then put the dough balls and sprinkle a little of cinnamon sugar mixture on top.

7. Put the mini loaf pan in air fryer and cook at 375F for 7 minutes

Allow to cool and SERVE!!

Mozzarella Cheese Sticks

Preparation time: 60 Minutes

Cook time: 10 Minutes

Servings: 6

Ingredients

- 1/2 Cup seasoned Italian breadcrumbs
- 6 Mozzarella cheese sticks
- 1/2 Cup of flour
- 1 Egg
- 3 Tablespoons of milk

Procedures

1. Cut the mozzarella cheese sticks into half.

2. Put the bread crumbs in one bowl, the flour in another bowl.

3. Mix the egg and milk in another bowl

4. Dip each of the cheese sticks first in the flour then egg and lastly in the breadcrumbs

5. Lay the Cheese sticks on a cookie sheet and put in the freezer until it is solid (about 1 - 2 hours)

6. Arrange the breaded sticks in the Air Fryer Basket

7. You can mist the sticks with cooking oil if you wish, for them to crisp up

8. Cook at 400 degrees for 10 minutes. (Cooking time varies depending on number of sticks)

Serve!!

Chanukkah Latkes

Preparation Time: 18 minutes

Cook Time: 9 minutes

Servings: 16

Ingredients

- 5 Large peeled Potatoes
- 1 Large (Yellow/Brown) Onion
- 1/2 Teaspoon of Baking Powder optional
- 4 Large Eggs
- 1/4 Cup Potato Starch (divided) optional
- 1/3 Cup of Matzo Meal
- 1/2 Teaspoon of Freshly Ground Black Pepper
- 2 Teaspoons of Salt
- Olive Oil

Procedures

1. Scrub the potatoes (peel if desired) and run through a food processor to grate. After grating, put in a bowl of water

2. Also grate the onions with the food processor. (Rinse Food processor, before grating onions). Place the onions in a paper towel to drain the water

3. Whisk the eggs in a bowl then add the salt, pepper, matzo meal, 1 TBL potato starch, baking powder (if any) and the grated onions

4. Drain the water off the potatoes and save the starch left in the bowl.

5. Drain out all the water from the potatoes and add them to the onion mixture

6. Scoop the Saved starch from the bowl and add it to the latkes mixture

7. Form the latkes into flat circles then dip inside the potato starch.

8. Spray all sides of the latkes generously with oil and also grease the Air Fryer basket with oil

9. Cook at 380 degrees for 9 minutes, flipping halfway through

Serve with desired sauce

Eggplant Parmesan

Preparation Time: 15 minutes

Cook Time: 25 minutes

Servings 4

Ingredients

- 1 Large eggplant about 1.25 lb.
- 1 Teaspoon of Italian seasoning mix
- 1/2 Cup whole wheat bread crumbs
- 1 Egg
- 1/4 Cup of mozzarella cheese, grated
- 1 Tablespoon water
- Salt as desired

- Fresh parsley for garnish
- 3 Tablespoon of whole wheat flour
- 3 Tablespoon of parmesan cheese, grated
- Olive oil spray
- 1 Cup of marinara sauce

Procedures

1. Cut the eggplant into 1/2" slices and rub some salt on both sides then leave for 12 minutes

2. While waiting, Mix the egg with water and flour in a small bowl to prepare the batter.

3. In a shallow plate, mix thoroughly the bread crumbs, parmesan cheese, Italian seasoning blend and little salt.

4. Add the batter to each eggplant slice evenly, dip the battered slices in the breadcrumb mix to coat it on all sides.

5. Put the (now breaded) eggplant slices on a dry flat plate then spray oil on the slices.

6. Preheat Air Fryer to 360F then put the eggplant and cook for about 9 mins

7. Top the Air fried slices with 1 tablespoon of the marinara sauce and lightly spread fresh mozzarella cheese on it.

8. Cook for another 2 mins to melt all the cheese

Serve with your Pasta.

Chicken Wings (Plain)

Preparation Time: 10 minutes

Cook Time: 15 minutes

Servings: 4

Ingredients

- 2 lbs. Chicken wings [cut into drumettes and flats]
- Cooking spray
- Black pepper ground
- Salt to taste

Procedures

1. Pat Chicken Wings dry and put inside a bowl

2. Season with the pepper and salt and mix well

3. Heat the Air Fryer to 350F and spray the basket with cooking spray

4. Cook Chicken wings in batches for 15 mins, flip after first 8 minutes

Note: Chicken must reach an internal temperature of 75 C (165F) before serving

Serve!

Chicken Wings (Parmesan)

Preparation Time: 10 minutes

Cook Time: 15 minutes

Servings: 4

Ingredients

- 2 lbs. Chicken wings [cut into drumettes and flats]
- Cooking spray
- 1 Teaspoon of Herbes de Provence
- 1 Teaspoon of paprika
- 1/2 Cup of grated Parmesan Cheese and a little extra to garnish
- Salt to taste

Procedures

1. Pat Chicken wings dry and put in a bowl.

2. Mix Parmesan, paprika, Herbes de Provence and salt

3. Coat the Chicken wings in the Parmesan Mix

4. Heat the Air Fryer to 350F and spray the basket with cooking spray

5. Cook Chicken wings in batches for 15 mins, flip after first 8 minutes

6. Garnish it with the extra Parmesan and fresh herbs

Note: Chicken must reach an internal temperature of 75 C (165F) before serving

Serve!

French Fries

Preparation Time: 60 minutes

Cook Time: 15 minutes

Serving: 6

Ingredients

- 3 Large russet potatoes
- 2-3 Tablespoons of olive oil
- Sea salt and pepper, to taste

Procedures

1. Slice the potatoes into fries using a Mandoline

2. Place our spuds in a cool water bath. Submerge the fries in the water completely

3. Allow the fries to sit for 60 minutes (1 hour).

Note: This removes excess starch and makes it crisp more in the Fryer

4. Preheat air Fryer to 375 degrees

5. Once 60 minutes is expired, drain the water and pat the fries dry with a paper towel

6. Toss the fries with the olive oil, salt and pepper

7. Add the fries to the Air Fryer basket, all on the same level. (Don't place them on each other)

8. Cook for 13 minutes until it is crispy and golden brown

9. Place it on a baking sheet (lined with paper towels and a cooling rack over it)

10. Put in a oven (with a maximum temperature of 250 degrees) and allow to rest while the other fries are cooking

Serve Hot!!!

Popcorn Chicken

Preparation Time: 30 minutes

Cook Time: 8 minutes

Servings: 4

Ingredients

For the Marinade

- 2 lbs. Chicken Breast Tenders
- 1/2 Ground Paprika
- 2 Cups of Almond Milk
- 1/2 Teaspoon of Black Pepper
- 1 Teaspoon of Salt

For the Dry

- 3 Cups of Flour
- Oil spray
- 3 Teaspoons of salt
- 2 Teaspoons of paprika
- 2 Teaspoon of black pepper

Procedures

1. Cut the Chicken into small pieces

2. Get a large zip lock bag and add the chicken and all the MARINADE ingredients.

3. Marinade in the Fridge for at least 2 hours to 6 hours.

4. Add the DRY ingredients in a large bowl

5. After Marinating, place the chicken and marinade into a large bowl and dredge the chicken chunks into the DRY ingredients in batches then dunk again into the marinade briefly. Dredge again in the DRY ingredients ensuring all piece of Chicken is fully coated

6. Grease the Air Fryer Bottom and sides with oil then place the breaded chicken in an even layer. Set aside the rest of the chicken.

7. Spray with olive oil the top of the Chicken in the Air Fryer vessel and place into the air fryer

8. Cook at 370 degrees for 8 minutes. Shake after first 4 minutes.

9. Remove then repeat process for all chicken

Serve Immediately

Orange Turkey Burgers

Preparation Time: 15 minutes

Cook Time: 11 minutes

Servings: 4

Ingredients

- 1 Pound Ground Turkey Beef (or Chicken)
- 1 Teaspoon (Dry/Ground) Mustard Seed

- 1/4 Teaspoon of Chinese Five Spice
- 1 Tablespoon of Old Fashion Oatmeal
- 1 Scallion, diced

INGREDIENT 2 (Orange Basting Sauce)

- 1/2 Cup of Orange Marmalade
- 2 Teaspoons of Oyster Sauce
- 1 Teaspoon of Premium Fish Sauce
- 1 Tablespoon of Soy Sauce

INGREDIENT 3 (Orange Aioli)

- 1 Teaspoon of Orange Zest
- 1/2 Cup of Mayonnaise
- 1 Teaspoon of Ground Chili Paste
- 1 Tablespoon of Orange Juice

Procedures

1. Whisk together INGREDIENT 3 and put inside the fridge

2. Mix INGEREDINT 2 also and set aside

3. Preheat the Air Fryer at 400 degrees for 10 minutes

4. Mix together the burger ingredients (first ingredients) plus 1tbsp of mixture 1 (baking sauce)

7. shape into 6 patties.

NOTE: Make an indentation in the center of each patties to keep it from puffing

8. Grease the Air Fryer basket with oil and place the Patties inside

9. Cook at 360 degrees for 9 minutes. baste burgers every 2 minutes.

10. After 6 minutes, turn the burgers over, flip over again, baste and cook for 3 minutes more

Serve Orange Aioli.

Persian Kabab Koobideh

Preparation Time: 8 minutes

Cook Time: 12 minutes

Servings: 3

Ingredients

- 2 Scallions
- 3 Cloves of Fresh Garlic
- 1/4-1/2 Cup of Plain Breadcrumbs
- 1 Pound of (Boneless) Chicken thighs and breasts
- 4 Ounces of (Yellow/Brown) Onion chopped
- 1 Tablespoon Lemon Juice
- 1/3 Cup of Fresh Flat Leaf Parsley
- 1 Large Egg
- 1/2 Teaspoon of Freshly Ground Black Pepper
- 1/4 Teaspoon of Turmeric Powder

For Finishing

- 1 Teaspoon Ground Sumac
- 1 Lemon
- 1 Cup Tzatziki Sauce Recipe

Procedures

1. Grate the onions inside a paper towel then squeeze out excess water. Squeeze again with another paper towel wrapped around the grated onions to remove the rest of the water

2. Put the chicken, Onions, 1/4 cup breadcrumbs, garlic, egg, pepper, parsley, turmeric, salt and lemon juice inside the food processor and process them until they are well combined

3. If the mixture is really wet, mix it in more Breadcrumbs

4. Put the chicken mixture in the freezer for 20 minutes.

5. Divide the mixture into 5 pieces and roll into 6" logs around the skewer

6. Grease Air Fryer basket with oil and place the Kabobs inside, spray well with oil and cook for 6 minutes at 400 degrees

7. Remove and carefully flip the Kabobs Koobideh and add tomatoes. Spray them with olive oil and cook for another 5 minutes (until the Kabobs are cooked through and the tomatoes are softened)

Place a Koobideh and a Tomato on each plate with Basmati Rice then drizzle a little fresh lemon juice and lemon zest over the food. Sprinkle sumac over the food on the plate.

Garlic Ranch Wings

Preparation time: 18 minutes

Cook Time: 25 minutes

Servings: 4

Ingredients

- 3 Tablespoons of Ranch Seasoning Mix
- 1/4 Cup of melted Butter
- 6 (quantity as desired) Cloves or Fresh Garlic minced (or more)
- 2 Pounds Chicken Wings

Procedures

1. Melt the butter and mix with the Ranch dry seasoning plus the garlic

2. Put the chicken wings in a container and pour in marinade. Put the container in the fridge for at least 4 hours (or overnight)

3. Put the chicken wings into the Air Fryer and cook for 20 minutes at 360 degrees. Turn twice during the cooking time.

4. Increase the temperature to 390 F and cook for additional 5 minutes

Nutritional Information: 411kcal | Fat: 31g | Carbs: 7g | Protein: 22g

SIDE DISH RECIPES

Cauliflower Rice

Preparation Time: 10 minutes

Cook Time: 20 minutes

Servings: 3

Ingredients

For the Tofu:

- 1/2 Extra Firm or Block Firm Tofu
- 1 Cup Diced Carrot (1 to 2 carrots)
- 2 Tablespoons Sodium Soy Sauce, reduced
- 1 teaspoon turmeric
- 1/2 cup onion, diced

For the Cauliflower:

- 3 Cups Riced Cauliflower (Cauliflower minced into pieces smaller than the size of a pea. This can be done with either a cheese crater or food processor or you get pre-riced cauliflower)
- 1 1/2 Teaspoons of toasted sesame oil
- 2 Tablespoons sodium soy sauce, reduced
- 1/2 Cup of broccoli, finely chopped
- 1 Tablespoon rice vinegar
- 1 Tablespoon ginger, minced
- 1/2 Cup Frozen peas
- 2 Cloves Garlic, minced

Procedures

1. Crumble the Tofu in a large bowl then toss with all the ingredients for the Tofu

2. Cook for 10 minutes at 370F, shake once.

3. Toss all the ingredients for the Cauliflowers in a large bowl.

4. After the tofu has air fried for 10 minutes, add the Cauliflower ingredients to the Air Fryer, shake gently and cook for 10 minutes at same temperature (370). Shake after every 5 minutes

5. You can cook for additional time as desired

Herbed Brussels Sprouts

Preparation Time: 10 mins

Cook Time: 8 mins

Serving: 4

Ingredients

- 2 Teaspoon of oil
- 1 lb. Cleaned and trimmed brussels sprouts

- 1/4 Teaspoon of salt
- 1 Teaspoon of dried parsley
- 1/2 Teaspoon of dried thyme
- 1 Teaspoon of garlic powder

Procedures

1. Put all the ingredients in a bowl and mix until the Brussels are sprouted evenly.

2. Put in the Air Fryer basket

3. Heat at 390 degrees Fahrenheit for 8 minutes.

4. Serve

Scotch Eggs with Spicy Pepper Sauce

Preparation Time: 20 mins

Cook Time: 25 mins

Servings: 4

Ingredients

- 1 Cup of Shredded Parmesan Cheese
- 2 Teaspoons of Coarse-ground Mustard
- 1 Pound of Bulk Pork Sausage
- 1 Tablespoon of Finely Chopped Fresh Chives
- 2 Tablespoons of Finely Chopped Fresh Parsley
- 1/8 Teaspoon of Freshly Grated Nutmeg
- 1/8 Teaspoon of Salt
- 1/8 Teaspoon of Ground Black Pepper
- 4 Hard Cooked of Peeled Eggs

Procedures

1. Combine the sausage, mustard, chives, nutmeg, salt, pepper and parsley in a large bowl and mix gently well combined.

2. shape the mixture into four equal-size patties and place each egg on a sausage patty then shape sausage around egg.

3. Dip each in shredded Parmesan cheese, press lightly and ensure the cheese shreds are well pressed into the meat.

4. Arrange eggs in the Air Fryer basket and spray lightly with nonstick vegetable oil.

5. Cook at 400F for 15 minutes, flip eggs and spray with vegetable oil after the first 7 minutes.

Serve with coarse ground Mustard.

Buffalo Chicken Bites

Preparation time: 2 minutes

Cook time: 10 minutes

Servings: 4

Ingredients

- Chicken thighs, boneless and skinless
- Salt to taste
- 2 Tablespoons of your favorite sauce

Procedures

1. Season the chicken thighs with salt

2. Air fry at 390F for 11 minutes

3. Once cooked, Remove from Fryer and toss immediately into the sauce

Chicken Coconut Meatballs

Preparation Time: 10 minutes

Cook time: 15 minutes

Servings: 4

Ingredients

- 2 Green Finely Chopped Onions
- 1 Pound of Ground Chicken
- 1 Tablespoon of Hoisin Sauce
- 1/2 Cup of Chopped Cilantro
- 1/4 Cup of Shredded Coconut, unsweetened
- Pepper, to taste
- 1 Teaspoon of sesame oil
- 1 Tablespoon of soy sauce
- 1 Teaspoon Sriracha
- Salt, to taste

Procedures

1. Mix all ingredients together gently giving a wet and sticky mixture.

2. Cook at 350F for 10 minutes, flip once until they reach an internal temperature of 150-165F

Serve

Avocado fries

Preparation Time: 10 minutes

Cook time: 10 minutes

Servings: 2

Ingredients

- 1/2 Teaspoon salt
- 1 Egg
- 1/2 Cup of Panko Bread Crumbs
- 1 Ripe but firm avocado

Procedures

1. Cut the Avocado into half and remove the pit. Cut into wedges

2. Beat the egg with salt in a bowl

3. Add the panko into a second bowl

4. First dip the avocado wedges into the egg mixture and then into the panko crumb

5. Preheat Air Fryer to 400F and put the wedges in a single layer for 8-10 minutes, shake after the first 5 minutes

5. Done when lightly brown

Serve

Buffalo Cauliflower Bites

Preparation Time: 5 minutes

Cook Time: 10 minutes

Servings: 3

Ingredients

- 1 Cup of Ranch Dressing
- 1 Egg
- 1 Cup Panko Crumbs
- 1/2 Cup of Hot Sauce
- 1/2 Teaspoon Powdered Garlic
- 1/2 Head Cauliflower
- 1/2 Teaspoon salt
- Freshly Ground Black Pepper

Procedure

1. Cut the Cauliflower into florets.

2. Dip them in the egg, mixed with salt, garlic powder and pepper. Lastly, dip into the panko breadcrumbs

3. Preheat Air fryer to 400 degree and add all the Cauliflower to the basket and cook for about 10 minutes. Shake after the first 5 minutes

4. Mix Ranch with hot sauce and serve on the side

Parmesan Meatballs

Preparation Time: 10 minutes

Cook Time: 15 minutes

Serving: 8

Ingredients

- 1 Tablespoon of Worcestershire Sauce
- 2 Pounds Ground Beef
- 1/3 Cup Italian Seasoned Panko Bread Crumbs
- 1/4 Cup Parmesan Cheese, grated
- 1/4 Cup Dried Onion, minced
- Chopped Fresh Italian Parsley (3 tablespoons)
- 1 Teaspoon Garlic, minced
- Salt & Pepper to taste
- 2 Eggs

Procedures

1. Mix all the meatball ingredients using a potato masher.

2. Grease the Air Fryer basket with oil and roll 2-inch sized meatballs and place them in a single layer in the air Fryer, without them touching.

3. Cook at 350F for about 13 - 15 minutes. (Cook time varies, check after first 12 minutes to see if done)

4. OPTIONAL: You can drizzle the meatball with marinara sauce and a little cheese in a dish and then put back in the Air Fryer for some minutes to melt

5. Serve as desired, either with spaghetti and marinara or sandwich.

Baked Potato - Baked Garlic Parsley Potatoes

Preparation Time: 5 minutes

Cook Time: 35 minutes

Servings: 3

Ingredients

- 1 Teaspoon of Parsley
- 1 Tablespoon of Salt
- 3 Idaho or Russet Baking Potatoes
- 1-2 Tablespoons of Olive Oil
- 1 Tablespoon of Garlic

Procedures

1. Create air holes with a fork in the potatoes after washing

2. Sprinkle the potato with the oil and seasoning, then rub the seasoning evenly on the potatoes

3. Place the Potatoes in the Air Fryer once they are coated

4. Cook at 392 degrees for 35-40 minutes or until fork tender.

Serve, topping with your favorite

Zero Oil Crispy Roasted Broccoli

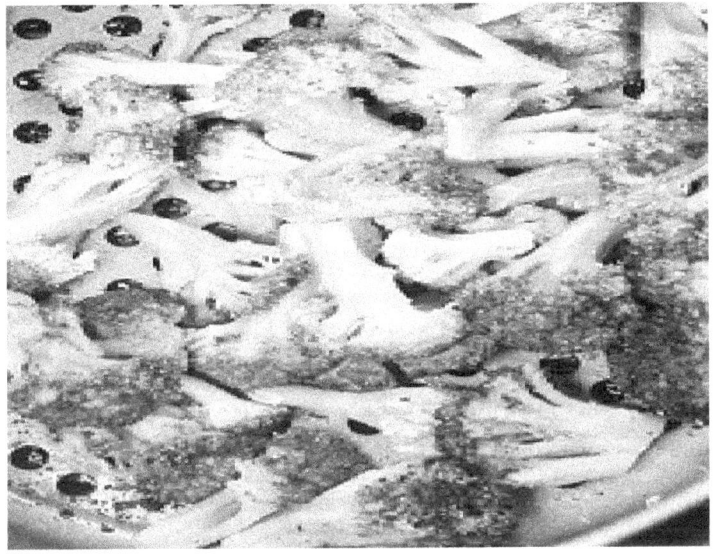

Preparation Time: 45 minutes

Cook Time: 10 minutes

Servings: 2

Ingredients

- 500 Grams Broccoli

For the Marinade:

- 1/4 Teaspoon of Masala Chat
- 1 Tablespoon of Chickpea Flour
- 2 Tablespoons of Yogurt
- 1/2 Teaspoon of Salt
- 1/4 Teaspoon of Turmeric Powder
- 1/2 Teaspoon of Red Chili Powder

Procedures

1. Cut the Roasted Broccoli into small florets and soak in a bowl of salty (2 teaspoon) water for 30 minutes to remove any form of impurities or worms

2. Once 30 minutes ins expired, remove the Broccoli from the water and drain well, also wipe using a towel to absorb the moisture

3. Mix all the marinade ingredients in a bowl and toss the broccoli into the mixture.

4. Cover and keep in the Fridge for 15 minutes

5. Preheat the Air fryer at 200C and place the Broccoli florets inside the Air fryer after it is marinated

6. Cook for 10 minutes. Shake after the first 5 minutes.

7. Once 10 minutes is expired, check to see if it is golden and crisp. If it is not, cook for another 3 minutes.

Serve Hot!!

Nutritional Information: 23kcal | Fat: 0g | Carbs: 6g | Protein: 1g

Corn on the Cob

Preparation Time: 2 minutes

Cook Time: 8 minutes

Servings: 2

Ingredients

- 2 Ears of Fresh Sweet (husk and silk removed, halved) Corn
- Salt and Pepper to taste
- 1 Tablespoon Oil

Procedures

1. Cut the Corn into half giving you four pieces

2. Gently pour the oil over the corn and rub in with your hands

3. Place the Corns into the Air Fryer Basket, cook at 380 degrees F and cook for 8 minutes. After the first 4 minutes, remove basket and shake.

4. After cooking time, carefully remove the corn. You can garnish with more salt and pepper if desired

Serve

Breaded Mushrooms

Preparation Time: 5 Minutes

Cook Time: 7 minutes

Servings: 2

Ingredients

- 80g of Grated Parmigiana Reggiano Cheese
- 250g of Button Mushrooms
- Flour
- 1 Egg
- Breadcrumbs
- Salt and Pepper

Procedures

1. Preheat Air Fryer to 360F

2. Mix the Breadcrumbs and cheese in a bowl

3. Beat the eggs in another bowl

4. Put half a cup of flour in another bowl

5. Wash Mushrooms and pat dry with kitchen paper

6. Roll each mushroom in the flour, dip in the egg then in the breadcrumbs and cheese mixture ensuring it is coated evenly

7 Once done with all mushrooms, place them in the Air Fryer basket and cook at 360F for 7 minutes. Shake basket after the first 3 minutes

SERVE!!!

Shrimp Toast (Chinese)

Preparation Time: 15 minutes

Cook Time: 4 minutes

Servings: 8

Ingredients

- 1/2 Teaspoon of Soy Sauce
- 1/4 Teaspoon of Pure Sesame Oil
- 1 Tablespoon of Fresh Flat Leaf Parsley
- 8 Ounces of Shrimp (deveined/peeled)
- 4-6 Slices of White Sandwich Bread
- 1 Large Egg
- 1 Tablespoon of Mayonnaise

- 1/4 Teaspoon of Premium Fish Sauce
- 2 Teaspoons of Potato Starch
- 1 Teaspoon of Fresh Ginger Root peeled
- Oil Mister
- Oil

Optional:

- 1/4 Cup of Natural Sesame Seeds
- 1/8 Teaspoon of Chili Paste

Procedures

1. Spray one side of the bread with oil and put inside the Air Fryer basket with the oil side up.

2. Cook at 370 degrees for 2 minutes, while it is cooking, add all the ingredients except the Sesame seeds to the bowl of Food Processor and process until it makes a paste

3. Remove the Bread from the Air Fryer then flip over; this time oil side faces down.

4. Spread the Shrimp paste over each bread slice evenly all the way to the edges

5. Place the Sesame seed to a flat plate and press the bread, shrimp side down into the sesame seeds

6. Cut each of the bread into 4 triangle and place it into the Air Fryer Basket

7. Shrimp paste side up, spray shrimp paste generously with oil

8. Cook for 5 minutes at 330 degrees (until the shrimp turns pink and the bread is no longer soft)

Salmon Croquettes (Jewish style)

Preparation Time: 55 minutes

Cook Time: 10 minutes

Servings: 6

Ingredients

3-14.75 ounces of Bumble Bee Pink Salmon (boneless and skinless / remove the skin and bones)

3 Tablespoons of Mayonnaise

2 teaspoons of Lemon Juice

2 Tablespoons of Matzo Meal

2 teaspoons of Italian Seasoning Grinder

1 medium grated Carrots

1 small Yellow/Brown grated Onion

2 large Eggs

1 Tablespoon of Chives chopped

Salt, to taste

1/4 Teaspoon of Freshly Ground Black Pepper

Procedures

1. Mix the Aioli and place in an air tight container in Fridge and place the Salmon in a medium bowl

2. Peel and grate the Carrot. Grate Onions also and squeeze out the excess water then add it to the bowl with Salmon

3. Add the Eggs, carrots, onions, Mayonnaise, Italian seasonings, chives, salt, Matzo meal, lemon juice, pepper and mix well

4. Form into 12 patties (3 inches in diameter) about 3/4-inch-thick then place in the fridge for at least 30 minutes

5. Grease the Air Fryer basket with oil and place the patties in a single layer.

6. Cook for 6 minutes at 400 degrees, flip over and spray again with oil then cook for additional 4 minutes

Garnish with chives and lemon zest then serve with Lemon Dill Aioli

Passover Matzo Taco Chips

Preparation Time: 4 minutes

Cook Time: 8 minutes

Servings: 4

Ingredients

- 1 Teaspoon Tomato Powder
- 1/4 Cup of Parmesan Cheese Parve, Grated
- 1/4 Teaspoon of Ground Cumin
- 5 Sheets of Matzo
- 1/4 Tablespoon of Paprika
- 1.5 Teaspoons of Chili Powder
- 1 Teaspoon of Sea Salt
- 1/4 Teaspoon of Powdered Garlic
- 1/4 Teaspoon of Powdered Onion
- Tiny Pinch of Pepper
- Olive Oil

Procedures

1. Mix all the ingredients together apart from the Oil (the last ingredient on the list)

2. Spray both sides of the matzo with the oil then break into Tortilla chip size pieces.

3. Put the Matzo in a bag and pour the seasoning inside then shake the bag to combine

4. Grease the air Fryer basket with oil and place the Matzo pieces inside. Place the Trivet over the Matzo

5. Cook for 8 minutes at 380 degrees until slightly brown and crisp

Allow to cool before serving

Garlic Bread Buns

Preparation Time: 5 minutes

Cook Time: 3 minutes

Servings: 4

Ingredients

- 1/8 Cup of Parmigiano-Reggiano Cheese, grated (or Asiago)

- 1/4 Cup of Fresh Minced Garlic
- 2 Hot Dog Buns
- 2 Tablespoons of Butter
- Paprika
- Dried Oregano

Procedures

1. Put a saucepan over a medium-low heat. Melt the butter in the saucepan then add the garlic. Sauté for 5 minutes

2. Open the hot dog buns (with inside facing up) then brush the butter over the cut side of the buns.

3. Spread the garlic on the buns and lightly sprinkle the Oregano and paprika on the Hot Dog Buns, one after the other. then add Asiago to the Buns

4. Place the Hot dog buns in the Air Fryer and cook for 3 minutes at 370 degrees

Serve

Sweet Potato Fries

Preparation Time: 5 minutes

Cook Time: 18 minutes

Servings: 2

Ingredients

- 1/2 Cup of Dipping Sauce as desired
- Seasoning Recipe to taste
- 2 Medium size Sweet Potatoes
- 3 TBL Potato Starch
- Coconut oil

Procedures

1. Slice the potatoes to 1/4".

2. Add the potato slices and potato starch in a Ziploc bag and shake well.

3. Remove the potato slices and shake off excess starch.

4. Place the Potato slice in a large bowl and coat it with the coconut oil. Sprinkle seasoning after that

5. Grease Air Fryer and place the potato slice inside then cook at 380 degrees for 20 minutes. Shake the basket after the first 10 minutes

Enjoy

Peanut Butter Banana Dessert Bites

Preparation Time: 15 minutes

Cook Time: 6 minutes

Servings: 12

Ingredients

- 1 Oil Mister
- 1 Large Banana
- 1/2 Cup Peanut Butter
- 12 Won Ton Wrappers
- 1-2 Teaspoon Vegetable Oil

Procedures

1. Slice the banana then place in a bowl of water, add a splash of lemon to prevent it from browning

2. Take each Banana slice and a teaspoon of peanut butter, place in the middle of won ton wrapper. Brush water along the edges of the wrapper

3. Bring together the opposite corners of the wrapper and squeeze, fold up the remaining opposite sides and squeeze.

4. Grease the Air Fryer basket with oil then place it in the Air fryer and spray generously with oil.

5. Cook at 380 degrees for 6 minutes

Serve with vanilla ice cream and a dusting of Cinnamon and sugar

CPSIA information can be obtained
at www.ICGtesting.com
Printed in the USA
LVHW110703040121
675640LV00024B/267

9 781691 187553